Transitions from Authoritarian Rule

Tentative Conclusions about Uncertain Democracies

by
Guillermo O'Donnell and
Philippe C. Schmitter

The Johns Hopkins University Press
Baltimore and London

9 8

The Johns Hopkins University Press
2715 North Charles Street
Baltimore, Maryland 21218-4363
www.press.jhu.edu

Library of Congress Cataloging-in-Publication Data

O Donnell, Guillermo A.
   Transitions from authoritarian rule. Tentative conclusions about
uncertain democracies.
   Papers originally commissioned for a conference sponsored by the
Latin American Program of the Woodrow Wilson International Center
for Scholars between 1979 and 1981.
   Bibliography: p.
   Includes index.
   1. Representative government and representation—Case
studies.   2. Authoritarianism—Case studies.   3. Democracy—
Case studies.   I. Schmitter, Philippe C.   II. Woodrow Wilson Inter-
national Center for Scholars. Latin American Program.
JF1051.0317   1986   321.09   86-2714
ISBN 0-8018-2682-9 (pbk. : alk. paper)

A catalog record for this book is available from the British Library.

Contents

Foreword

Abraham F. Lowenthal

The three coeditors of *Transitions from Authoritarian Rule* have kindly invited me to introduce this effort because it resulted from the Woodrow Wilson Center's project on "Transitions from Authoritarian Rule: Prospects for Democracy in Latin America and Southern Europe."

The "Transitions" project was the most significant undertaking of the Wilson Center's Latin American Program during the seven years I had the privilege of directing its activities. The resulting four-volume book contributes substantially on a topic of vital scholarly and political importance. I want to highlight both these points, to underline some of its strengths, and finally to say a bit about what is still left to be done.

The Woodrow Wilson International Center for Scholars was created by an act of the United States Congress in 1968 as a "living memorial" to the twentieth president of the United States, a man remembered for his idealism and for his commitment to democracy, for his scholarship, for his political leadership, and for his international vision, but also for his interventionist attitudes and actions toward Latin America and the Caribbean. The Center supports advanced research and systematic discussion on national and international issues by scholars and practitioners from all over the world. It aims to bring together the realms of academic and public affairs, as Wilson himself did.

The Latin American Program was established early in 1977, within the Center's overall framework, to focus attention on the Western Hemisphere. The Program has tried, from the start, to serve as a bridge between Latin Americans and North Americans of diverse backgrounds, to facilitate comparative research that draws on the Center's special capacity to bring people together, to emphasize the highest standards of scholarship, to stress privileged topics that merit intense cooperative efforts, and to help assure that opinion leaders in the United States and Latin America focus more attentively and more sensitively on Latin America and the Caribbean and on their relation with the United States.

In all its undertakings, the Program has been striving to assure that diverse viewpoints—from men and women with varying national, professional, disciplinary, methodological, and political perspectives—are presented, and that complex issues are illuminated through the confrontation of different analyses. But the Program's orientation has never been value-free; it has stood for vigorous exchange among persons who disagree about many things but who fundamentally respect the academic enterprise and who share a commitment to the core values all the nations of the Americas profess. The Program has sought diversity of many kinds, but not artificial balance. It awarded fellowships in the same semester to writers exiled because of their convictions from Argentina and from Cuba, for example, but it has never invited their censors on an equal basis. It has sponsored research on human rights from many different standpoints, but never from the perspective of the torturers. And it sponsored the project on "Transitions from Authoritarian Rule" with a frank bias for democracy, for the restoration in Latin America of the fundamental rights of political participation.

The "Transitions" project was begun in 1979 on the initiative of two charter members of the Latin American Program's nine-person Academic Council: Guillermo O'Donnell (then of CEDES in Buenos Aires) and Philippe Schmitter (then of the University of Chicago), with the active encouragement and support of the Council's chairman, Albert O. Hirschman, and of Council member Fernando Henrique Cardoso of Brazil. During the project's first phase, I served as its coordinator. As the project grew in scope and complexity, it became clear that another Center-based person was needed to focus more fully on it; we were fortunate to recruit Laurence Whitehead of Oxford University, a former Wilson Center fellow, who then worked closely with O'Donnell and Schmitter and became coeditor of the project volume.

The "Transitions" project illustrates the Wilson Center's aspirations in several respects:

Its leaders are recognized as among the world's foremost academic authorities in Latin America, the United States, and Europe.

It attracted the participation of other top-flight scholars from all three continents and encouraged them to work closely together in a structured and linked series of workshops and conferences.

It emphasized comparative analysis, and sharpened the focus on Latin American cases by putting them into a broader perspective.

In its various workshops, the project drew on the perspective not only of scholars but of several persons—from Latin America and from among former U.S. government officials—experienced in politics and public affairs.

Its findings have been made available to opinion leaders from different sectors through specially organized discussion sessions in Washington.

It maintained a creative tension between its normative bias, its theoretical ambitions, and its empirical and case-oriented approach. The project's animus, as I had occasion to say at its first meeting, was never wishful thinking but rather "thoughtful wishing," that is, it was guided by a normative orientation that was rigorous and deliberate in its method.

Finally, the project illustrated a point the Wilson Center's director, Dr. James H. Billington, has often emphasized: to seek tentative answers to fundamental questions rather than definitive responses to trivial ones. All the project's participants know that the complex issues involved in transitions to democracy have not been dealt with conclusively in this volume, but they can take great satisfaction in what they have contributed.

Transitions from Authoritarian Rule

Ultimate evaluations of this book's import, obviously, will have to come from analysts less involved in the project's inception and management than I. I would like, however, to suggest some of the reasons why I think *Transitions from Authoritarian Rule* is important.

It is the first book in any language that systematically and comparatively focuses on the process of transition from authoritarian regimes, making this the central question of scholarship as it is today in Latin American politics.

Its analytic and normative focus on the prospects of building democratic or polyarchic politics in the wake of an authoritarian transition provides a vantage point that organizes the materials in ways useful not only to scholars and observers but to political actors as well.

Its comparisons of cases in Latin America and in Southern Europe and of cases of transition from bureaucratic authoritarianism, military populism, and sultanistic despotism allow for considering several different variables.

Transitions from Authoritarian Rule is rich in nuanced, contextually sensitive analysis, and each of the case studies is written by a leading authority. Although the methods, perspectives, and styles of the various authors understandably differ, their agreement on shared assumptions makes this a coherent volume. The book is filled with subtleties, complexity, and a keen sense of paradox.

Throughout, disaggregation is emphasized. All authoritarian regimes are not equated with each other. No authoritarian regime is regarded as monolithic, nor are the forces pushing for democratization so regarded. Distinctions are drawn between "democracy" and "polyarchy"; between "democratization" and "liberalization"; between "transition" and "consolidation"; between "hard-liners" and "soft-liners" or accommodationists within the authoritarian coalition; and among "maximalists," "moderates," and "opportunists" in the coalition supporting *abertura* (liberalization).

From the various cases, several points emerge that deserve special mention here. These cases show that, although international factors, direct and indirect, may condition and affect the course of transition, the major participants and the dominant influences in every case have been national. They demonstrate the importance of institutions, of mediating procedures and forums that help make the rules of political discourse legitimate and credible in a period of change. They illustrate the vital significance of political leadership and judgment, of the role of single individuals in complex historical processes. They point out, again and again, the importance of timing, the complexity of inter-active processes carried out over extensive periods, the various ways in which transitions produce surprises, and some of the ironies and paradoxes that result.

Above all, the cases analyze the ways in which transitions from authoritar-ian rule are conditioned and shaped by historical circumstances, unique in each country but patterned in predictable ways, by the way in which a pre-vious democratic regime broke down, by the nature and duration of the authoritarian period, by the means the authoritarian regime uses to obtain legitimacy and to handle threats to its grip on power, by the initiative and the timing of experimental moves toward *abertura*, by the degree of security and self-confidence of the regime's elites and by the confidence and competence of those pushing for opening the political process, by the presence or absence of financial resources, by the counseling of outsiders, and by the prevailing inter-national *fashions* that provide legitimacy to certain forms of transition.

The Tasks Ahead

I do not wish to detain the reader longer before he or she enters the reading of *Transitions from Authoritarian Rule*. It remains only to concede, as all the authors would, that this book is incomplete, and that much remains to be done. The cases of transition are still few in number, and each one merits a much more detailed and sustained analysis. The processes of consolidation, so important if these transitions are to be meaningful, are barely considered in this volume, and require separate treatment. The sensitivity that the authors in their chapters show to the dilemmas and choices faced by opposition groups pressing for *abertura* needs to be matched by equally empathetic and well-informed assessments of the choices made by those within authoritarian regimes who permit *abertura* to occur and push for its extension. Some of the categories of analysis—of hard-liners (*duros*) and soft-liners (*blandos*), for example—need to be further specified and refined.

All this and more needs to be done. No doubt the editors and authors of *Transitions from Authoritarian Rule* will be among the leaders in carrying out this research. Some of them will be leaders, as well, in the very processes of building democracies. They, and many others, will go much further than this volume can, but they will build upon a solid foundation.

Preface

Between 1979 and 1981 the Latin American Program of the Woodrow Wilson International Center for Scholars, in Washington, D.C., sponsored a series of meetings and conferences entitled "Transitions from Authoritarian Rule: Prospects for Democracy in Latin America and Southern Europe." As this project grew in scope and complexity, Abraham Lowenthal, program secretary from 1977 to 1983, provided indispensable encouragement that enabled us to turn it into the present four-volume study. We wish to acknowledge our special debt of gratitude to him, and also to thank the Woodrow Wilson Center, the Aspen Institute for Humanistic Study, the Inter-American Foundation, the Helen Kellogg Institute of the University of Notre Dame, the European University Institute in Florence, and Nuffield College, Oxford, for their financial and logistical support. Louis Goodman, acting secretary of the Latin American Program in 1983–84, also gave us much-needed assistance. Needless to add, only those named in the table of contents are responsible for the views expressed here.

All of the papers published in these four volumes were originally commissioned for a Woodrow Wilson Center conference or were circulated, discussed, and revised in the course of the "Transitions" project. They have, therefore, some commonality of approach and outlook, but it was never our intention to impose a uniformity of interpretation and terminology. On the contrary, we deliberately set out to widen the range of serious discussion about regime transitions in general, and to promote informed debate comparing specific cases. In Volume 4, O'Donnell and Schmitter present the lessons they have drawn from this experience of collaboration among scholars working on Latin America and Southern Europe. Volume 3 contains a series of discussion papers analyzing common themes from different perspectives. Volume 1 (on Southern Europe) and Volume 2 (on Latin America) contain country studies, some of which were written during or immediately after the launching of a democratic transition, and some even before it had begun. Two cases (Uruguay and Turkey) were added to our sample at a later stage in the project as developments in these countries called for their inclusion, whereas the chapter on Italy refers to a transition completed more than thirty years earlier. Because of these differences in timing, and the delay in publication, readers should be warned that not all chapters carry the analysis right up to date (end of 1984).

Although the three editors are listed alphabetically in volumes 1, 2, and 3, they, of course, established some division of labor among themselves. Primary responsibility for Volume 1 rests with Philippe C. Schmitter; Laurence Whitehead took the lead in editing Volume 2; and Guillermo O'Donnell had first responsibility for Volume 3. This has been very much a collective endeavor, however, and all three of us share credit or blame for the overall result.

Transitions from Authoritarian Rule

Tentative Conclusions about Uncertain Democracies

1 •

Introducing Uncertainty

The present volume deals with transitions from certain authoritarian regimes toward an uncertain "something else." That "something" can be the instauration of a political democracy or the restoration of a new, and possibly more severe, form of authoritarian rule. The outcome can also be simply confusion, that is, the rotation in power of successive governments which fail to provide any enduring or predictable solution to the problem of institutionalizing political power. Transitions can also develop into widespread, violent confrontations, eventually giving way to revolutionary regimes which promote changes going far beyond the political realm.

The contributors to this project have approached their respective tasks from perspectives which reflect their own values and preoccupations, as well as the often distinctive characteristics of the countries and issues that they are confronting. We have respected this diversity, regarded it as desirable, and tried to learn from it. Nevertheless, in our coordination of the project we have tried to accentuate three general and shared themes, which we believe are sufficient to ensure as reasonable a degree of convergence as is warranted by the considerable variety of empirical material and the paucity of prior theoretical guidelines. We did not have at the beginning, nor do we have at the end of this lengthy collective endeavor, a "theory" to test or to apply to the case studies and thematic essays in these volumes.

The first general and shared theme is normative, namely, that the instauration and eventual consolidation of political democracy constitutes per se a desirable goal. Some authors may have been more sensitive than others to the trade-offs that this may imply in terms of forgone or deferred opportunities for greater social justice and economic equality, but we all agreed that the establishment of certain rules of regular, formalized political competition deserved priority attention by scholars and practitioners.

The second theme, to a certain extent a corollary of the first, involves an effort to capture the extraordinary uncertainty of the transition, with its numerous surprises and difficult dilemmas. Few moments pose such agonizing choices and responsibilities, ethical as well as political. If we ever have the temerity to formulate a theory of such processes, it would have to be a chapter in a much larger inquiry into the problem of "underdetermined" social change, of large-scale transformations which occur when there are insufficient structural or behavioral parameters to guide and predict the outcome. Such a theory would have to include elements of accident and unpredictability, of crucial decisions taken in a hurry with very inadequate information, of actors facing irresolvable ethical dilemmas and ideological confusions, of dramatic turning points reached and passed without an understanding of their future significance. In other words, it would have to be a theory of "abnormality," in which the unexpected and the possible are as important as the usual and the probable. Moreover, the actors' perception of this very abnormality surrounding regime change is itself a factor affecting its eventual outcome. Compared to periods of "order" which characterize the high point of authoritarian rule, the uncertainty and indirection implied in movements away from such a state create the impression of "disorder." This impression some compare nostalgically with the past, while overlooking or regretting the transition's revival of precisely those qualities which the previous regime has suppressed: creativity, hope, self-expression, solidarity, and freedom.

The third theme is closely related to the one we have just discussed. When studying an established political regime, one can rely on relatively stable economic, social, cultural, and partisan categories to identify, analyze, and evaluate the identities and strategies of those defending the status quo and those struggling to reform or transform it. We believe that this "normal science methodology" is inappropriate in rapidly changing situations, where those very parameters of political action are in flux. This includes transitions from authoritarian rule. The increasingly free expression of interests and ideals following liberalization, the variations and shifts in the configuration of power and benefit within the authoritarian regime, and the high indeterminacy of interactions, strategies, and outcomes are, among other characteristics we shall discuss below, crucial reasons for the inadequacy of using "normal" social science concepts and approaches to analyze such situations. During these transitions, in many cases and around many themes, it is almost impossible to specify *ex ante* which classes, sectors, institutions, and other groups will take what role, opt for which issues, or support what alternative. Indeed, it may be that almost all one can say is that, during crucial moments and choices of the transition, most—if not all—of those "standard" actors are likely to be divided and hesitant about their interests and ideals and, hence, incapable of coherent collective action. Moreover, those actors are likely to undergo significant changes as they try to respond to the changing contexts presented them by liberalization and democratization. We believe, therefore, that this type of situation should be analyzed with distinctly political concepts, however vaguely delineated and difficult to pin down they may be. This is not meant to be a methodological credo, advocating the exclusive use of "strategic" concepts heavily weighted toward political calculations and immediate reactions to unfolding processes. Rather, we have attempted to shape conceptual tools that may be reasonably adequate for dealing with choices and processes where assumptions about the relative stability and predictability of social, economic, and institutional parameters—and, therefore, of their descriptive and explanatory power—seem patently inadequate. Nor is this a denial of the long-run causal impact of "structural" (including macroeconomic, world systemic, and social class) factors. It is, to repeat ourselves on a point that we would like not to be misunderstood, our way of recognizing the high degree of indeterminacy embedded in situations where unexpected events (*fortuna*), insufficient information, hurried and audacious choices, confusion about motives and interests, plasticity, and even indefinition of political identities, as well as the talents of specific individuals (*virtù*), are frequently decisive in determining the outcomes. This is not to deny that the macrostructural factors are still "there," as we shall see at several points in this volume. At some stages in the transition, in relation to certain issues and actors, those broad structures filter down to affect the behavior of groups and individuals. But even those mediations are looser, and their impacts more indeterminate, than in normal circumstances. The short-term political calculations we stress here cannot be "deduced" from or "imputed" to such structures—except perhaps in an act of misguided faith.

As the participants agreed at the beginning, the motivation of this project, and now of the publication of its results, has been practical as well as contemplative. In terms of the latter, the challenge was to explore a theme as uncharted as it is intriguing, taking advantage of the generous support of the Latin American Program of the Woodrow Wilson International Center for Scholars of the Smithsonian Institution, and its unprecedented willingness to bring together a working group of distinguished scholars from the United States, Europe, and Latin America. On the side of *praxis* we believe that by exposing the "state of our ignorance," enriched by our reflections about typical dilemmas and choices, and by some generalizations about typical processes, we are providing a useful instrument—pieces of a map—for those who are today venturing, and who tomorrow will be venturing, on the uncertain path toward the construction of democratic forms of political organization. All of us who have participated in this project hope that at least it will contribute to a more intelligent and better-informed discussion, by activists and scholars, of the potentialities, dilemmas, and limitations involved in the complex process of the demise of authoritarian rule and its *possible* replacement by political democracy.

Defining Some Concepts (and Exposing Some Assumptions)

One major difficulty confronting our collective effort was to create a common language for inquiry among scholars with rather heterogeneous backgrounds. While we cannot pretend to have resolved it completely—many words continue to be used diversely in the chapters of these volumes—the participants did agree on the significance of certain key concepts, and in so doing, they exposed some shared assumptions. These we will try to capture in the following pages.

Transition

What we refer to as the "transition" is the interval between one political regime and another.[1] While we and our collaborators have paid some attention to the aftermath (i.e., to consolidation), our efforts generally stop at the moment that a new regime is installed, whatever its nature or type. Transitions are delimited, on the one side, by the launching of the process of dissolution of an authoritarian regime and, on the other, by the installation of some form of democracy, the return to some form of authoritarian rule, or the emergence of a revolutionary alternative. It is characteristic of the transition that during it the rules of the political game are not defined. Not only are they in constant flux, but they are usually arduously contested; actors struggle not just to satisfy their immediate interests and/or the interests of those whom they purport to represent, but also to define rules and procedures whose configuration will determine likely winners and losers in the future. Indeed, those emergent rules will largely define which resources can legitimately be expended in the political arena and which actors will be permitted to enter it.

Moreover, during the transition, to the extent that there are any effective rules and procedures, these tend to be in the hands of authoritarian rulers. Weakly or strongly, depending on the case and the stage of the transition, these rulers retain discretionary power over arrangements and rights which in a stable democracy would be reliably protected by the constitution and various independent institutions. The typical sign that the transition has begun comes when these authoritarian incumbents, for whatever reason, begin to modify their own rules in the direction of providing more secure guarantees for the rights of individuals and groups.

Liberalization

The process of redefining and extending rights we have labeled "liberalization." It is indicative of the beginning of the transition that its emergence triggers a number of (often unintended) consequences which play an important role in ultimately determining the scope and extension of that process. By liberalization we mean the process of making effective certain rights that protect both individuals and social groups from arbitrary or illegal acts committed by the state or third parties. On the level of individuals, these guarantees include the classical elements of the liberal tradition: habeas corpus; sanctity of private home and correspondence; the right to be defended in a fair trial according to preestablished laws; freedom of movement, speech, and petition; and so forth. On the level of groups, these rights cover such things as freedom from punishment for expressions of collective dissent from government policy, freedom from censorship of the means of communication, and freedom to associate voluntarily with other citizens.

Granted that this complex of guarantees has probably never been totally and unconditionally observed by public authorities in any country, and that its content has changed over time, movement along these lines, however sporadic and uneven, constitutes an important departure from the usual practice of authoritarian regimes. As Adam Przeworski observes in his chapter in Volume 3, such movements have the effect of lowering the costs—real and anticipated—of individual expression and collective action. This, in turn, has a multiplier effect. Once some actors have dared to exercise those rights publicly and have not been sanctioned for doing so as they were during the zenith of the authoritarian regime, others are increasingly likely to dare to do the same. There does not appear to be any necessary or logical sequence to the emergence of these "spaces" for liberalized action, although the reacquisition of some individual rights generally precedes the granting of guarantees for collective action. Nor are progressions in these domains irreversible. On the contrary, a characteristic of this early stage in the transition is its precarious dependence upon governmental power, which remains arbitrary and capricious. If, however, those liberalized practices are not too immediately and obviously threatening to the regime, they tend to accumulate, become institutionalized, and thereby raise the effective and perceived costs of their eventual annulment. This brings us to the relation between liberalization and the central concern of our analysis, democratization.

Democratization

Democracy's guiding principle is that of *citizenship*. This involves both the *right* to be treated by fellow human beings as equal with respect to the making of collective choices and the *obligation* of those implementing such choices to be equally accountable and accessible to all members of the polity. Inversely, this principle imposes *obligations* on the ruled, that is, to respect the legitimacy of choices made by deliberation among equals, and *rights* on rulers, that is, to act with authority (and to apply coercion when necessary) to promote the effectiveness of such choices, and to protect the polity from threats to its persistence. There have been a great variety of decision-rules and procedures for participation claiming to embody the citizenship principle. Across time and political units, the actual institutions of democracy have differed considerably. No single set of specific institutions or rules by itself defines democracy, not even such prominent ones as majoritarianism, territorial representation, legislative sovereignty, or popularly elected executives. Indeed, many institutions now thought of as distinctively democratic were initially set up with very different intentions, and were only subsequently incorporated within its reigning definition, for example, parliaments, parties, mixed governments, interest groups, consociational arrangements, and so on. What specific form democracy will take in a given country is a contingent matter, although given the existence of certain prominent "models" and international diffusion, there is likely to exist a sort of "procedural minimum" which contemporary actors would agree upon as necessary elements of political democracy. Secret balloting, universal adult suffrage, regular elections, partisan competition, associational recognition and access, and executive accountability all seem to be elements of such a consensus in the contemporary world. On the other hand, other institutions, such as administrative accountability, judicial review, public financing for parties, unrestricted access to information, limitations on successive terms in office, provisions for permanent voter registration and absentee balloting, compulsory voting, and the like, might be considered as less essential, or as experimental extensions of the citizenship principle in more advanced, more "complete" democracies.

Democratization, thus, refers to the processes whereby the rules and procedures of citizenship are either applied to political institutions previously governed by other principles (e.g., coercive control, social tradition, expert judgment, or administrative practice), or expanded to include persons not previously enjoying such rights and obligations (e.g., nontaxpayers, illiterates, women, youth, ethnic minorities, foreign residents), or extended to cover issues and institutions not previously subject to citizen participation (e.g., state agencies, military establishments, partisan organizations, interest associations, productive enterprises, educational institutions, etc.). As is the case with liberalization, there does not seem to be any logical sequence to these processes, although some regional and temporal patterns can be discerned. Nor is democratization irreversible; indeed, all of the countries included in these volumes have had some of these rules and procedures in the past, so that recuperation is often as important a goal as extension and expansion.

Notes on the Interaction of Liberalization and Democratization

As we have defined them above, liberalization and democratization are not synonymous, although their historical relation has been close. Without the guarantees of individual and group freedoms inherent in the former, the latter risks degenerating into mere formalism (namely, the so-called popular democracies). On the other hand, without the accountability to mass publics and constituent minorities institutionalized under the latter, liberalization may prove to be easily manipulated and retracted at the convenience of those in government. Nevertheless, during the transition the two may not occur simultaneously. Authoritarian rulers may tolerate or even promote liberalization in belief that by opening up certain spaces for individual and group action, they can relieve various pressures and obtain needed information and support *without* altering the structure of authority, that is, without becoming accountable to the citizenry for their actions or subjecting their claim to rule to fair and competitive elections; in the literature this form of rule has occasionally been given the euphemistic label of "tutelary democracy." In our discussions we referred to such cases as "liberalized authoritarianism" (*dictablandas*). Inversely, once democratization has begun and its prudent advocates fear the excessive expansion of such a process or wish to keep contentious issues off the agenda of collective deliberation, they may well continue old, or even create new, restrictions on the freedoms of particular individuals or groups who are deemed insufficiently prepared or sufficiently dangerous to enjoy full citizenship status. For these cases we invented the term "limited democracy" (*democraduras*).

Based on these distinctions we venture the following generalizations:

1. Liberalization is a matter of degree even if it is not, strictly speaking, measurable according to a common scale for all cases. It can be more or less advanced, depending on the scope of its guarantees, as well as on the extent to which persons and groups can obtain rapid and effective protection against eventual violations.

2. Democratization also admits of gradations, although again, we find it difficult to specify, out of time and national context, what rules and procedures would be more or less democratic. In the formation of a *political* democracy (i.e., one that restricts the application of the citizenship principle to public institutions of governance) two dimensions seem particularly important, however. One refers to the conditions that restrict party competition and electoral choice—for example, banning certain political parties or ideological currents, fixing prohibitively high thresholds for their formation, restricting admissible candidacies, rigging constituency boundaries and overrepresenting particular districts and interests, and/or limiting the means of party finance. The other dimension refers to the eventual creation of a "second tier" of consultative and decisional mechanisms, more or less explicitly designed to circumvent accountability to popularly elected representatives by placing certain issues out of their reach—for instance,

establishing autonomous parastate agencies, corporatist assemblies, and/or consociational arrangements. Democracy itself may be a matter of principles, but democratization involves putting them into practice through specific and detailed rules and procedures, which quite often have effects far beyond their seemingly microscopic significance.

3. Liberalization can exist without democratization.[2] Fundamental guarantees can be accorded while impeding individuals or groups from participation in competitive elections, from access to policy deliberations, and/or from exercising the rights that may make the rulers reasonably accountable to them. This is frequently justified on the grounds that "immature" subjects must be tutored before they can be allowed the exercise of full citizen responsibilities. Nevertheless, the cases studied in these volumes suggest that once some individual and collective rights have been granted, it becomes increasingly difficult to justify withholding others. Moreover, as liberalization advances so does the strength of demands for democratization. Whether these will be strong enough to compel such a shift and yet not too strong (or too premature, in terms of the field of forces given at any moment in the transition) to provoke an authoritarian regression is one of the major uncertainties of the transition.

4. In all the experiences examined, the attainment of political democracy was preceded by a significant, if unsteady, liberalization. Admittedly, in some cases—Portugal and Greece—the transition was so rapid that the two were almost contemporaneous, but even there, crucial individual and collective rights were made effective before the convocation of competitive elections, the organization of effective interest representation, and the submission of executive authority to popular accountability. Therefore, it seems useful to conceptualize the overall transition as a sort of "double stream" in which these two subprocesses interact over time, each with its own hesitancies and reversions, and each with overlapping motives and constituencies. In the event of a successful outcome (i.e., viable political democracy) the two become securely linked to each other.

5. If liberalization begins the transition, then we can locate the *terminus ad quo* of our inquiry at the moment that authoritarian rulers (or, more often, some fraction thereof) announce their intention to extend significantly the sphere of protected individual and group rights—and are believed. Prior to this, a certain degree of de facto liberalization may have emerged, especially in contrast to the arbitrary "excesses" which tend to characterize the immediate aftermath of an authoritarian seizure of power, but this is likely to be a function of circumstance, inattention, or plain weariness on the part of the agents of repression. What is important is not just the expression of a subjective awareness on the part of the rulers that something must change (often with the Lampedusan coda, "if things are going to remain the same. . . ."), but the reception of this announcement by others. In other words, the intention of liberalizing must be sufficiently

credible to provoke a change in the strategies of other actors. This permits us to exclude from the *problématique* of the transition actions by authoritarian incumbents intended either to ratify or to transform certain of the characteristics of the regime, even when these take the form of a "popular consultation." The Pinochet plebiscite in Chile in 1980 is a case in point, although this strategy can backfire, as did the plebiscite in Uruguay and, in a somewhat different way, the 1974 electoral upset in Brazil. This criterion also permits us to identify abortive transitions in which the announced intention to protect some rights is either withdrawn by its proponents or canceled by rival factions within the regime.

6. One premise of this way of conceptualizing the transition is that it is both possible and desirable that political democracy be attained without mobilized violence and dramatic discontinuity. The threat of violence and even frequent protests, strikes, and demonstrations are virtually always present, but where the *vía revolucionaria* is taken, or when violence becomes widespread and recurrent, the prospects for political democracy are drastically reduced. To use the terms suggested in Schmitter's original essay, a "transfer of power," in which incumbents hand over control of the state to some faction of their supporters, or a "surrender of power," where they negotiate the transition with some of their nonmaximalist opponents, seems more propitious for the installation and consolidation of democracy than an "overthrow of power" by implacable antagonists.[3] For most of the cases in point, the latter scenario has been a simple impossibility, despite occasional terrorism and armed insurrection, given the military capacity of those in government and the unwillingness of the population to support such an uncertain and costly adventure. Nicaragua was the exception among the cases discussed at our 1980 conference, where Richard Fagen suggested why the Somoza regime left virtually no alternative for regime transformation.[4] Gianfranco Pasquino's chapter on Italy at the end of World War II shows that even where armed insurrection did occur and its partisans controlled substantial portions of the country, the decision not to press forward—the famous "Svolta di Salerno" by Togliatti—made a crucial difference in that transition.

Socialization

The advent of political democracy is the preferred *terminus ad quem* of our interpretive effort, but it is not the end of struggles over the form and purpose of politics. As Adam Przeworski argues in his chapter, democracy institutionalizes uncertainty, not only with respect to the persons and groups who will occupy positions of authority, but also with respect to the uses to which authority will eventually be applied. In a sense, the transition to political democracy sets up the possibility—but by no means, the inevitability—of another transition. For the citizenship principle of equal treatment in matters affecting collective choices knows no intrinsic boundaries, except those set, at a given moment, by tradition, received wisdom, explicit agreement, or countervailing power. De Tocqueville was perhaps the first to grasp the powerful potentialities of this fact and to glimpse the possibility that once applied to the procedures of public government, it could also be extended in two directions: (1) to cover other, "private" social institutions; (2) to demand that not merely formal equality of opportunity but also substantive equality of benefits be attained.

At the risk of confusing the term with other uses in the social sciences, we have called this "second" transition "socialization." It also involves a double stream, two independent but interrelated processes. The one, which some label "social democracy" consists of making the workers in factories, the students in schools and universities, the members of interest associations, the supporters of political parties, the clients of state agencies, even the faithful of churches, the consumers of products, the clients of professionals, the patients in hospitals, the users of parks, the children of families, etc., *ad infinitum*, into citizens—actors with equal rights and obligations to decide what actions these institutions should take. The other process, at times associated with the term "economic democracy," relates to providing equal benefits to the population from the goods and services generated by society: wealth, income, education, health, housing, information, leisure time, even autonomy, prestige, respect, and self-development. Their simultaneous presence or attainment is what is meant here by "socialization," and this remains a powerful hope for many actors. Whether these processes are, or can be made, compatible with each other—whether equal participation in the units of social action would entail equal distribution of the benefits from collective choices, and vice versa—is indeed one of the major, unanswered questions of our time. Certainly the experience of both the modern welfare state and "real-existing socialism" shows that more equal public provision of services and availability of goods does not always encourage higher levels of citizen participation—and can even lead to recipient passivity, clientelistic structures, and dependence upon experts and administrators. Inversely, higher levels of participation in some institutions, through such devices as workers' councils and corporatist forums, can result in an increase rather than a decrease in the overall inequality of benefits, as each sector or unit seeks maximum returns for itself and passes off the costs to others.

For our purposes, the persistent (if remote) goal of socialization has a double relevance. On the one hand, the attainment of a relatively stable mix of liberalization and democratization—what Robert Dahl has called "polyarchy"[5]— may have the effect of freezing existing social and economic arrangements. This is most obviously the case where the basis of the compromise rests on mutual recognition of income shares and property rights. On the other hand, the aspiration to socialism leads some actors to expect that the transition from authoritarian rule will lead in relatively short order to widespread substantive benefits for all and to the destruction of the nondemocratic arrangements that

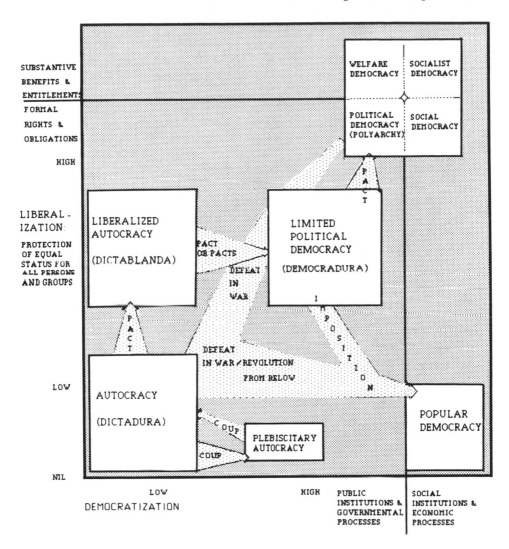

persist in private and semipublic institutions. In the contemporary world, these two transitions—to political democracy and to socialism—are simultaneously on the agenda. There will always be "radicals" advocating the desirability of leaping to the latter without pausing for the former, as well as "reactionaries" arguing that, by transiting to the former, societies are starting inevitably on a slippery slope toward the latter.

In this context, all we can do is reaffirm our earlier presumption that political democracy per se is a goal worthy of attainment, even at the expense of forgoing alternate paths that would seem to promise more immediate returns in terms of socialization. Not only is the probability of their success much lower and the likelihood of their promoting an authoritarian regression much higher, but the taking of such paths seems to require, at least in the interim, the installation of a popular authoritarian regime which is unlikely to respect either the guarantees of liberalization or the procedures of political democracy. Even leaving aside the predictable reaction of external powers to countries which take such a route (see the arguments advanced by Laurence Whitehead in Chapter 1 of Volume 3 and the actions presently being taken by the United States to "destabilize" the Nicaraguan revolution), it is by no means clear whether such a *vía revolucionaria* will in the long run be more successful than incrementally and consensually processed change in making socialization compatible with the values embodied in liberalization and political democracy.

For the convenience of the reader, in Figure 2.1 we have attempted to display graphically the "property-space" involved in the interaction between liberalization and democratization, as well as their possible supersession by socialization. The area of predominant concern in this volume is bounded on the vertical dimension by individual and collective rights and obligations, and on the horizontal one by public institutions and governmental processes. Within it, we identify two intermediate regime configurations (*dictablanda* and *democradura*), and several transition paths (involving defeat in war, revolution from below or without, or negotiation through successive pacts) which will be discussed in later chapters.

3 ·

Opening (and Undermining) Authoritarian Regimes

The Legitimation Problem

During the interwar period, authoritarian rulers could aspire to legitimate their government through some combination of the mobilizing imagery of Fascism and references to more traditional forms of corporatism. Such regimes could (and did) promote themselves as long-term solutions to the problems of political order and as the best possible modes of governance for their societies, especially when compared to impotent and divided parliamentary democracies elsewhere in Europe and to the prepotent and monolithic regime in the Soviet Union. Authoritarian rulers emerging after 1945 have not been able to count on such a possibility. This is their Achilles' heel, and it explains their ideological schizophrenia. They are regimes that practice dictatorship and repression in the present while promising democracy and freedom in the future. Thus, they can justify themselves in political terms only as transitional powers, while attempting to shift attention to their immediate substantive accomplishments—typically, the achievement of "social peace" or economic development.

The often haphazard attempts of these regimes at institutionalizing themselves clash with the limits imposed by their own discourse. These limits are, in part, imposed by the contemporary worldwide "marketplace" of ideas and, also, by enduring domestic aspirations, both of which imply that legitimate political domination can only be the expression of popular sovereignty or, in exceptional cases, the issue of a revolutionary mandate for dramatic social transformation. Under these conditions, the usual flurry of decree-making and law generation, as well as the bureaucratic expansion, of authoritarian regimes may increase their immediate capacity for control (and repression), but such efforts are not likely to be considered, even by incorporated and benefited social actors, as permanent arrangements. As for those sectors of the population that are excluded and victimized, the schizophrenic stamp of the regime opens the ideological space within which they can express what often becomes their fundamental demand: the removal of the authoritarian regime and its replacement by a democratic one.

"Hard-Liners" and "Soft-Liners"

In this context we must analyze the relationships between two groups typically present in such regimes: in the vocabulary of O'Donnell's original essay for this project, "hard-liners" (*duros*) and "soft-liners" (*blandos*).[1] The first are those who, contrary to the consensus of this period of world history, believe that the perpetuation of authoritarian rule is possible *and* desirable, if not by rejecting outright all democratic forms, then by erecting some facade behind which they can maintain inviolate the hierarchical and authoritarian nature of their power. These hard-liners are usually composed of several factions. Some adopt this position out of opportunism, indifferent to longer-term political projects, and preoccupied instead with their own survival in office and retaining their share of the spoils. Were these the only hard-liners, the task of transition would be largely a matter of determining the cost of buying them out at the right moment. But the main core of the hard-liners is formed by those who reject viscerally the "cancers" and "disorders" of democracy and who believe they have a mission to eliminate all traces of such pathologies from political life. Once a transition has begun, and even after political democracy has been established, this nucleus of unconditional authoritarians is likely to remain the stubborn source of attempted coups and conspiracies.

As for the soft-liners, they may be indistinguishable from the hard-liners in the first, "reactive"[2] phase of the authoritarian regime. They may be equally disposed to use repression and to tolerate the arbitrary acts of the appropriate ministry or security agency. What turns them into soft-liners is their increasing awareness that the regime they helped to implant, and in which they usually occupy important positions, will have to make use, in the foreseeable future, of some degree or some form of electoral legitimation. To this the soft-liners add that, if its eventual legitimation is to be feasible, the regime cannot wait too long before reintroducing certain freedoms, at least to the extent acceptable to moderate segments of the domestic opposition and of international public opinion.

But the timing of the first serious attempts at liberalization poses a typical paradox that greatly weakens the prospects for regime incumbents during the transition. The most favorable occasions for attempting liberalization come at periods of widely acknowledged success of the authoritarian regime, including a high economic conjuncture, in which the soft-liners hope that the regime's effectiveness will be transferred into popular support for the regime during the transition. But these are the periods during which the soft-liners are likely to find less support for—and to be less self-convinced of—their goals. If things are going well, and no important crises or challenges are foreseen, why decide on changes that will inevitably introduce new actors and uncertainties, however tightly liberalization may be controlled by the regime? Why risk the "achievements of the regime" for the sake of the fuzzy long-term advantages advocated by the soft-liners? This is the typical argument used by hard-liners, technocrats, and many others who prefer to continue enjoying the perquisites of unchallenged authoritarian rule, against the soft-liners—if the latter dare to express their views at all before such unpropitious publics. Thus, these regimes lose their golden opportunity to liberalize under the conditions that would maximize their chances for exercising close and enduring control over the transition. Of course, there have been authoritarian regimes, such as the 1976–83 Argentine one, which could hardly miss the opportunity, since they experienced during their entire duration very few "successes." But even those regimes attempted liberalization only when they were already going through some serious crisis, perceived as such by at least some of the regime incumbents and—most importantly—by the entire opposition.[3]

In any case, when liberalization is attempted, the innovations initially introduced by the regime rarely go beyond highly controlled (and often indirect) consultations and the restitution of some individual rights (not extensive to social groups or opposition parties). But even under such limited circumstances, soft-liners distinguish themselves from hard-liners by proclaiming that some form of democracy is the necessary outcome of the authoritarian episode that they "unfortunately" had to impose. In the vocabulary of Schmitter's original essay, they have begun to accept the "dispensability" of the regime and its incumbents. But like the hard-liners, the soft-liners are themselves composed of diverse currents. Some have gotten what they wanted from authoritarian rule and are prepared to withdraw to the enjoyment of private satisfactions. Others wish to see the transition stop at a limited liberalization which protects their tenure in office or their privileged access to authority. Still others aspire to elected positions in the emergent regime and are prepared to undertake the risk of leading down the trail to political democracy.

Thus, different orientations toward political order and political time have a subtle, but not insignificant, importance even before the transition begins. Moreover, the motives and circumstances under which an authoritarian regime came to power can have a lasting effect on its eventual outcome. The hard-liners tend to have more weight in the initial phases, all the more so where the threat and preceding crisis have been the most severe.[4] This implies a tendency for a greater and more systematic use of repression and the probability that there will be a more extensive effort to eradicate the institutions of previous democratic experiences. Even in such an unfavorable context, however, soft-liners do eventually emerge with their recognition that, at some time in the future, some kind of political "opening" will be necessary. At that point, some of the excluded actors will have to be allowed to reenter political life—however purged of "extremists" and "intransigents"—and this will be all the more difficult the longer harsh repression and violation of rights are practiced. Hence, even in the very moments when the regime's discourse seems most monolithic and cohesive, these elements of differentiation are likely to have appeared and to have sent out ambiguous signals to potential allies and real opponents.

The Context for Transitional Openings

As Philippe Schmitter, Laurence Whitehead, and others have pointed out, the most frequent context within which a transition from authoritarian rule has begun in recent decades has been military defeat in an international conflict. Moreover, the factor which most probabilistically assured a democratic outcome to the transition was occupation by a foreign power which was itself a political democracy.[5] On the other hand, in spite of the Greek fiasco in Cyprus, and until the Malvinas/Falklands war caught us by surprise, the deus ex machina of military defeat seemed unlikely for the cases which interested us. Italy was an exception among our cases, and Gianfranco Pasquino shows that the Allied invasion and subsequent occupation played a key role there. Portugal represented a partial exception, in the sense that the impending defeat of its colonial pretensions was a major factor in bringing down the authoritarian regime. But even there, as Kenneth Maxwell's chapter indicates, domestic conflicts and motives were important factors in the regime's inability to defend itself against what was, after all, initially a putsch by a small group of junior army officers.

In all the other cases, the reasons for launching a transition can be found predominantly in domestic, internal factors. Of course, ideological constraints at the international level have some effect on actor perceptions of the long-term viability of a given regime, and the negative impact of a downturn in the international economy can accelerate matters. Nevertheless, it seems to us fruitless to search for some international factor or context which can reliably compel authoritarian rulers to experiment with liberalization, much less which can predictably cause their regimes to collapse. Even if one seizes upon the impact of military fiascos such as the Malvinas/Falklands for Argentina and Cyprus for Greece, it is more accurate to interpret them as the result of an already tottering and stalemated regime launching a *fuite en avant* rather than as the cause for the regime's having reached such an impasse.

In this sense our explorations took a rather different turn from those which have attempted to explain the advent of the very authoritarian regimes whose demise—actual or potential—was the object of our interest. This is somewhat ironic, given the fact that several of the participants in our project (one of the coauthors included) were active protagonists in the research and discussions generated by attempts to account for the emergence of those authoritarian regimes.[6] This may be a sign of intellectual flexibility—or of theoretical fuzziness. But in our opinion, it is basically a recognition that political and social processes are neither symmetric nor reversible. What brings down a democracy is not the inverse of those factors that bring down an authoritarian regime—and the same can be said for the successful consolidation of these respective regime types. Political democracies are usually brought down by conspiracies involving few actors (even though, usually at later stages, those actors may obtain mass support for their efforts), and this may give special leverage to external manipulations and calculations. The liberalization and eventual democratization of authoritarian regimes may have its conspiratorial side, but it also involves, as we shall see, a crucial component of mobilization and organization of large numbers of individuals, thereby attenuating the role of external factors.

But the main reason for this asymmetry springs from the themes and assumptions we stated at the beginning of this volume, that is, the high degree of indeterminacy of social and political action and the inordinate degrees of freedom that collective and even individual action may have at some momentous junctures of the transition. Hope, opportunity, choice, incorporation of new actors, shaping and renewal of political identities, inventiveness—these and many other characteristics of the politics of the transition stand in sharp contrast to the mode and tone of politics in the periods preceding the breakdown of democratic regimes. One of the basic arguments (which we share) of the Juan Linz and Alfred Stepan volume to which we have just made implicit reference,[7] is that none of those breakdowns was fatalistically bound to occur, that is, they could have been avoided if some strategic decisions had been made and especially if some crucial mistakes had not been committed. This, however, does not detract from the fact that crucial *personae* during the breakdown period seem in retrospect like actors in a Greek tragedy, anticipating their fate but fulfilling it to the bitter end, powerless either to modify their solidarities, alliances, and styles, or to control the international, macroeconomic, macrosocial, and institutional factors that led toward the breakdown. In contrast, the uncertainties, risks, and deficits of information characteristic of the transition away from authoritarian rule have as their counterpart a context of expanding (if uncertain) choices, of widespread (if often exaggerated) hopes, of innumerable (if seldom finally institutionalized) experiments toward the expansion of the political arena,[8] and of manifold levels of social participation. What actors do and do not do seems much less tightly determined by "macro" structural factors during the transitions we study here than during the breakdown of democratic regimes. The dismayed impotence of most democratic political actors during the latter contrasts sharply with what gives a characteristic flavor to many moments of the transition—namely, the exultant feeling (even if it is usually quite exaggerated) that the future is open, and that ideals and decisions count as much as interests and structures. Even by itself, this strong belief is likely to be a powerful factor, in the short and medium run, for reinforcing the high degree of structural indeterminacy that characterizes such moments.

Leaving these speculations aside, let us return to our statement that domestic factors play a predominant role in the transition. More precisely, we assert that there is no transition whose beginning is not the consequence—direct or indirect—of important divisions within the authoritarian regime itself, principally along the fluctuating cleavage between hard-liners and soft-liners. Brazil and Spain are cases of such a direct causality. In those two countries, the decision to liberalize was made by high-echelon, dominant personnel in the incumbent regime in the face of a weak and disorganized opposition. Portugal offers a slight variant on this scenario, in that the "openers" came from the middle echelon of the military, who were quickly compelled by the ensuing spontaneous popular mobilization not just to liberalize but to democratize. In Greece, Peru, and Argentina circa 1970, the "decision to open" was heavily influenced by the presence of strong opposition forces in the civilian population. Nevertheless, several putschs and purges had to occur, in the government and in the armed forces, before the soft-liners acquired sufficient control over governmental and military positions to be able to implement such a decision.

Nor can the timing of an opening toward liberalization be correlated predictably with the performance of authoritarian rulers in meeting socioeconomic goals. Both relative success and relative failure have characterized these moments, although admittedly, standards are highly subjective, and evaluations are likely to differ both inside and outside the regime. Most cases fall somewhere in the middle, but it is interesting to contrast Brazil and Spain, on the one hand, with Peru, Greece, and Argentina. In the latter cases, not just opponents but most of those within the regime concluded that the experience of authoritarian rule was a resounding failure even according to the standards the regime itself had established. Opponents were stimulated to act because the failure was so obvious. Ruling groups, including the armed forces, were less and less confident of their own capacities, as well as deeply fragmented by recriminations over who was responsible for the regime's failures. Mediators were no longer willing to arbitrate dissent and hold coalitions together. Faced with this, the authoritarian rulers sought a rapid "political outlet" (*salida política*). This gave ample room to the soft-liners, for whom it seemed less risky to launch the country into liberalization, and even democratization, than to continue struggling inflexibly and ineffectively against a rising tide of opposition, fed by defection from the regime's ranks.

In contrast, authoritarian regimes that had been relatively successful and hence had encountered a less active and aggressive opposition opted for the transition with a higher degree of self-confidence. Hoping that they could put together a comfortable majority, they aimed at attaining electoral ratification and popular legitimation for what has always been the most sensitive internal management problem for authoritarian rulers, namely, succession to top executive office. In addition, they expected to earn a nice bonus in the eyes of international public opinion by following through on their original claims to be preparing the country for a return to democracy. Admittedly, as already noted, such decisions usually disguise important and rising tensions within the ruling coalition, as the chapters of both Luciano Martins and Fernando Henrique Cardoso show was the case in Brazil since practically the inception of this regime. Not only were some of the Brazilian military led to prefer liberalization by their own factionalism, but in the early 1970s part of the bourgeoisie opted for limited democratization out of concern over the expansion and growing autonomy of state agencies which had accompanied economic growth during the previous authoritarian decade. In Spain, a business class similarly favored by authoritarian rule was also prepared to support a transition from it, even more so since it was seen as a requisite to eventual entry into the European Community—but the exact timing of its occurrence was contingent upon a specific event, the death of Francisco Franco. Even with these peculiarities, the general point remains: those regimes that felt themselves successful were those in which the decision to embark on a transition was taken without a high degree of prior internal disaggregation or external pressure.

As O'Donnell notes in the Introduction to the volume on Latin America, the military-populist authoritarian regime in Peru had goals and social bases quite different from the other experiences we have examined. Also, it applied only moderate repression and made few changes in habitual patterns in this regard. Similarly, the experiment in bureaucratic-authoritarian rule which began in 1966 in Argentina was characterized by a low level of previous threat, the ambiguous role played by Peronism and the unions in their initial support for the coup, and by high expectations that "social peace" and development would be relatively easy to achieve; hence, the level of repression was relatively low.[9] In both cases, policy failures led to generalized dissatisfaction, and the regime lost control of the agenda and timing of the transition. This suggests that where dissent is high and regime self-confidence low, unless the cost of organizing collectively is raised (i.e., unless the hard-liners are prepared to invest more and more in repression, which may well be a self-defeating proposition), the transition will be imposed by a mobilized opposition. In such cases, the latter is likely to have comparatively high influence over the rules and issues of the transition. Conversely, no transition can be forced purely by opponents against a regime which maintains the cohesion, capacity, and disposition to apply repression. Perpetuation in power or armed revolutionary struggle become the only likely outcomes of such cases. On the other hand, where the cost of acting in dissent is rather low, but the objective performance and subjective confidence of the regime are high, a transition is not likely to occur, and when it does, it is bound to be restricted initially to rules and issues which the authoritarian rulers feel they can control.

None of these generalizations exclude the possibility of *accidents de parcours* in even the most carefully crafted of transitions, especially with regard to electoral results. Nevertheless, the regime-confident, self-initiated scenario differs from the opposition-induced one in two key respects: (1) the sequence, rhythm, and scope of liberalization and democratization tend to remain more firmly in the control of incumbents (and, therefore, occur more slowly and with less generalized uncertainty); and (2) the social and political forces which supported the authoritarian regime stand a better chance of playing a significant electoral and representational role in the subsequent regime.

The Preauthoritarian Legacy

Another important element differentiating the cases in these volumes concerns the extent to which representative institutions—political parties, social movements, interest associations, autonomous agencies, local governments—have survived from the period prior to authoritarian rule. In some cases, the longevity of such regimes and/or the ruthlessness with which they eradicated national political institutions and local autonomies meant that the transition faced almost a *tabula rasa*. Portugal is a case in point, and Manuel Antonio Garretón argues in his chapter that a similar situation might occur in Chile in the event of a liberalization-democratization of the Pinochet dictatorship. In other cases, usually of shorter duration, the structures and even the personnel inherited from the previous democracies have shown a surprising capacity for revival. Brazil and Peru are examples of this. Even in Italy, where the Fascists were in power for over twenty years, the king, the military, and even the Fascist Grand Council played a crucial role—for good and for ill—in ensuring some continuity during the transitional period, as Gianfranco Pasquino shows. In Spain, the institutions and legislation of the Franco regime, with roots in previous Spanish experience, were of major importance. The Cortes, its personnel unchanged, committed the extraordinary act of voting its own extinction and opening the way for the establishment of democratic institutions. In addition, the person of the king and the institution of the crown were essential in providing a central focus which consistently supported the transition and was accepted by almost all as being above party, faction, and particular interests.

Ironically, the more episodic and incoherent authoritarian experiences of Latin America, as well as that of Greece, seem to have done more to undermine the institutions of the more-or-less democratic regimes which preceded them than the longer-lived and ideologically stronger authoritarianisms of Italy, Spain, and Portugal. The former regimes have often destroyed previous institutions and practices without replacing them with alternative forms of representation, decision-making, or policy implementation. This may testify more to the greater resiliency of civil society in Southern Europe than to the inefficacy of authoritarian rulers in Latin America. Additional factors seem to be extreme fear of the "chaos" which preceded authoritarian rule in Latin America and the much stronger military component in these countries as compared with Italy, Portugal, and even Spain, which probably made them more hostile to any form of civilian political representation.

In this respect, Brazil is an interesting exception. As was the case with Argentina, Chile, Peru, Greece, and all other recent cases elsewhere, no serious attempt was made in Brazil to create distinctively authoritarian institutions. Rather, the generals who have governed Brazil since 1964 had the good sense to rule largely by distorting rather than by disbanding the basic institutions of political democracy. Previous parties were banned, but their quasi-resurgence was tolerated under the all-embracing rubrics of an official two-party system. Parliament was periodically closed down and had little to do with legislation and policy-making, but it did function most of the time and gradually acquired effective authority. Candidacies were controlled, but elections were held fairly regularly, especially at the local level, where competition remained lively. Thus, by the time the liberalization (*abertura*) was signaled by the relaxation of censorship in 1972, and then launched with the 1974 elections, some channels of organized political expression were already in place. Admittedly all this was carefully monitored by the regime, regressions did occur when "undesirable" results happened or even seemed likely, and the transition has gone much slower than elsewhere. Nevertheless, the role of representative institutions grew steadily, to the point that opposition parties became heavily represented in Congress[10] and controlled several important state governorships. Nevertheless, until 1984, they were denied the opportunity to compete under democratic rules for the highest national executive office.

Most of the other cases analyzed in these volumes have been different. The institutional context has had to be invented and learned almost *ex novo*. Authoritarian incumbents, having failed to create new institutions or to conserve old ones, have found themselves facing uncertain futures and dim prospects for protecting what they consider to be their vital interests. Regime opponents, having been given virtually no role within the authoritarian scheme of governance and, in some cases, having returned from exile to act in societies which have undergone substantial changes, often have had to rely on precarious past identities, outmoded slogans, and unimaginative combinations.

Once liberalization has been chosen—for whatever reason and under whatever degree of control by incumbents—one factor emerges which hangs like a sword of Damocles over the possible outcome. This is the fear of a coup that would not only cut short the transition but impose a regression to an even more restrictive and repressive mode of governance.

Fearing the Present

If there is one characteristic common to all our cases it is the omnipresent fear, during the transition, and often long after political democracy has been installed, that a coup will be attempted and succeed. Yet with the exception of Bolivia and the rather special case of Turkey, such coups did not occur during the transitions we have studied. There have been uncountable conspiracies and not a few failed attempts, but none of our other transitions was interrupted by a successful coup.

Why, then, has this nonevent received so much attention and generated so much anguish? In part, the question itself provides the answer: by being obsessed with its probable occurrence, contending forces in the transition take steps to prevent such an outcome and avoid taking decisions which they feel might encourage it. Obviously, this double negativity—the coup that doesn't happen and the actions not taken which could have encouraged it to happen—is most difficult to examine empirically. But there is subjective evidence from the actors themselves with which one can gain a better understanding of this crucial problem.

The possibility of a coup is not fictitious. Many groups within a declining or defunct regime—and not just military ones—are initially opposed to an opening, and become even more so once the conflicts and uncertainties it generates manifest themselves. These actors, the hard-liners, fear that the transition and political democracy are bound to lead to an abyss, and are prepared to force at any cost a return to the "good old times" of "order," "social peace," and "respect for authority." However secretly they may conspire, their existence and activities are known to the proponents and supporters of transition. However divided these proponents and supporters may be on substantive and procedural issues, they share an overriding interest in avoiding a coup. Indeed, this provides a crucial convergence, which may lead to explicit or implicit cooperation among these actors.

The impending coup poses difficult choices, especially to those pressing for full-fledged political democratization. They may feel it imperative to prevent or discourage the mobilization and the politicization of issues by groups which could be their crucial allies in the medium and long term but whose activity could constitute the *casus belli* that might trigger the coup. But how can those who want to push the transition avoid a coup without becoming so paralyzed by fear of it that they will disillusion their supporters and diminish their ability to press for further steps in the transition? Indeed, if they pursue this anticipated reaction too far, the promoters of the coup will have achieved their objectives without having acted: the transition will remain limited to a precarious liberalization, and the regime opponents will end up divided and deluded. Faced with such a dilemma, there does not appear to be a formula correct for each case and every conjuncture, but it is important to keep in mind the shifting strategic context. This will occupy us in the following pages.

Playing Coup Poker

Typically, at the beginning of the transition the soft-liners within the regime have a strong hand in relation to the opposition, the more so to the degree that they feel successful in having attained past goals. Their ace in the hole is the threat that if the opposition refuses to play according to the rules they propose initially—usually a modest liberalization confined to individual rights and a restricted democratization with tight limits on participants and a narrow agenda of permissible policy issues—they will simply cancel the game and return to the authoritarian *status quo ante*. This tends to weaken and divide the proponents of further democratization. Some believe the threat and, preferring to avoid the worse outcome, agree to play the soft-liners' game. Others prefer the risk of a showdown to accepting such a self-limited outcome. But, despite the initial strengths and intentions of the soft-liners their hand will eventually be recognized for the bluff that it has become. What forces the cards to the table is the growing evidence that, if a coup does indeed occur, the hard-liners will not only have to repress the regime's opponents but will also have to overthrow the soft-liners within its ranks. The factionalism of the regime is likely to increase to the point that the soft-liners come to recognize the interest they share with the opposition in avoiding a return to full-fledged authoritarian rule, even if the transition turns out to extend beyond the political forms and policy issues they initially tried to impose. Moreover, by continuing with the transition, the soft-liners can keep alive the hope that they will eventually be able to control the process and protect their interests. (This is the other side of the uncertainty of democracy; it can lead to self-limiting, conservative outcomes as well as to expansive, progressive ones.) Furthermore, if the transition results in the implantation of democracy, the soft-liners will not only be protected from the accusations of treachery laid on them by the hard-liners, but also be rewarded by "history" for having led their country to an arguably more honorable future. As Albert Hirschman has noted,[11] passions, even virtuous ones, can be as important as interests, and—we would add—concern for future reputation can be as powerful a motive as the desire for immediate satisfaction.

These factors generate a subtle but effective, and most often implicit, "first-order understanding"—the foundation of eventual pacts—between soft-liners and those in the opposition who are preeminently interested in the installation of political democracy. Of course, this does not mean that the two tacit allies will not continue to struggle with each other. But it does imply that their conflicts will tend to attenuate and to shift more and more to procedural rules and substantive restrictions. Once the soft-liners' bluff has been called, their manipulation of the specter of a coup becomes less direct and threatening. They then argue that if the opposition exceeds certain limits, this will strengthen the hand of the hard-liners in their coup attempts and/or in the competition for positions in the governing and military hierarchies that could be decisive for the rhythm and extent of the transition. But, as we shall see, this is very complicated, too.

That those who begin the transition by threatening a coup become the principal guarantors against such an outcome is one of the numerous paradoxes of our theme. But for this guarantee to be effective, the skills and machinations of the soft-liners may not be enough. It is crucial that among them, in a prominent role, should be found well-placed and professionally respected military officers. Just as the literature on the execution of coups stresses the role of "swingmen" at crucial conjunctures,[12] so the (nonexistent) literature on noncoups should emphasize the strategic importance of "swingmen" in making alternative outcomes possible. These officers may support the transition much more because of what they believe is good for the armed forces than because of any enthusiasm for democracy. In any case, their weight within the armed forces means that a coup will have to be made against them and in the face of armed forces that are likely, for that very reason, to be deeply divided. This makes the launching of a coup quite risky and its outcome predictably less successful, especially if we consider the numerous military officers who are opportunistic in their political options; they basically wish to come out on the winning side, and when in doubt about the odds they are more likely to support the existing situation than rebellious alternatives. We shall return to this theme.

The Cycle of Mobilization

But the real importance of these choices internal to the regime and to the armed forces can be appreciated only when they are related to concomitant developments in the opposition camp. The "opening," "thaw," "decompression," or whatever it is called, of authoritarian rule, usually produces a sharp and rapid increase in general politicization and popular activation—"the resurrection of civil society," as O'Donnell has described it. However, this wave crests sooner or later, depending on the case. A certain normality is subsequently reasserted as some individuals and groups depoliticize themselves again, having run out of resources or become disillusioned, and as others deradicalize themselves, having recognized that their maximal hopes will not be achieved. Still others simply become tired of constant mobilization and its intrusion into their private lives. These "shifting involvements"[13]—first with depoliticized life under the authoritarian regime, then with rapid and strong politicization during the first periods of the transition, and, later on, with a return to some form of relatively depoliticized citizenship (which may be, as it was in Spain, temporarily reactivated for the defense of democracy from hardline threats)—are typical of the processes we studied. The inverted U-shaped curve formed by the strike rate in the Spanish case represents this pattern graphically and can be repeated with many other indicators of mobilization and protest in all our cases. In terms of the strategies of hard-liners and soft-liners, those three periods have differing significance. First, at the onset of the transition, before most actors have learned that they can act at lower cost to themselves and their followers and, therefore, before an explosion of opposition has occurred, the soft-liners may well believe (and convince others) that they have and can keep control of the transition. The hard-liners then find it difficult to enlist support, since most of their potential recruits prefer to wait and see if the soft-liners can deliver their promise of retaining control while at the same time achieving a postauthoritarian political formula that will be more enduring and more acceptable domestically and internationally.

In the second period, when conflicts and "disorder" reach their zenith, the hard-liners' worst fears may be confirmed, and their capacity to recruit "fence-straddlers" increases. Then the conditions seem favorable for the coup that would produce the feared authoritarian regression. This is when the soft-liners are forced, for the reasons already noted, to reveal their predominant interest in preventing such an outcome. On the other hand, the greater the mobilization and protest of the opposition, the more obvious to the promoters of the coup that more extensive and systematic repression will be necessary. This implies not merely returning to the *status quo ante* but to some very extreme version of authoritarian rule, in which, quite obviously, the soft-liners will lose their present positions. The hard-liners may not have serious objections to applying the kind of repression that such authoritarian regression implies. But in order to do so, they and their would-be supporters need to count on the one element that the very existence of the soft-liners denies to them—a high degree of cohesion within the armed forces.

It follows that, contrary to the wishes of the soft-liners and the advice of almost everyone, the regime's opponents should increase their activity instead of prudently diminishing it, as the feared moment of the coup seems to approach. In particular, they should promote the diversification and extension of opposition throughout society, since that increases the perceived costs of repression for the hard-liners. However, we are confronted with one of those tricky, parabolic, if not sinuous relationships in which only good political judgment can test the limits of a situation. If the opposition menaces the vertical command structure of the armed forces, the territorial integrity of the nation-state, the country's position in international alliances, or the property rights underlying the capitalist economy, or if widespread violence recurs, then even bland regime actors will conclude that the costs of tolerance are greater than those of repression.[14] In such situations, the longer-term benefits of an eventual liberalization (not to mention democratization) will seem to those actors much less appealing than the shorter-term security of an immediate return to authoritarian rule.

Adding to the uncertainty of such calculations is the fact that the capacity for tolerating disorder and threats varies by class and sector of each society, and by historical period. What is regarded as an "insult to the armed forces," an "act of secession," or a "threat to property" is hardly a constant. Nor is it possible to specify a priori how specific social sectors will interpret the situation and react. One class condition which does seem unavoidable for the viability of the transition is that the bourgeoisie, or at least important segments of it, regard the authoritarian regime as "dispensable" in Schmitter's terms, either because it has laid the foundations for further capitalist development or because it has demonstrated its incompetence for doing so. Should the mobilization of regime opponents seem to go "too far," however, then authoritarian rule may again be judged to be indispensable, if unfortunate. Moreover, as was suggested by the study of the breakdown of democracy,[15] an authoritarian inflection by a large part of the bourgeoisie is usually accompanied by another symptom of impending danger: the mobilization of middle sectors in favor of a coup that will bring "order" to society. This class convergence, along with suitably inclined elements within the armed forces, is a necessary—if not sufficient—condition for a successful authoritarian seizure of power, against both a democratic regime and a transitional one.

By the time the third, or relatively demobilized, phase is reached, the capacity for tolerance of diverse actors has increased. Soft-liners and indecisive elements within the already defunct regime, as well as the social classes and sectors which supported it, have come to countenance conflicts and demands, modifications in the rules of the game and institutional arrangements, as well as levels and patterns of popular demands and organization they would never have accepted at the beginning of the transition—and have found that they can live with them. This is another way of illustrating that the transition involves continuous, if not linear or irreversible, modifications in both the relations of force between diverse actors and the conceptions they have about their interests.

But our analysis of this complex process of dissuasion, threat, and learning cannot advance further without tackling the problem which most contaminates the ethical and political climate of the transition and which, because of its reverberations within the armed forces, feeds the worst fears of a brutal regression. This is the problem of dealing with the repressive acts perpetrated during the authoritarian regime.

Settling a Past Account (without Upsetting a Present Transition)

In the cases analyzed here, the respective authoritarian regimes applied, at least for some period of their existence, severe and consistent coercion to broad segments of the population, and even more systematic and focused repression to particular parties, organizations, and individuals which they held responsible for the "chaos and corruption" that preceded their seizure of power. But behind this generalization lie significant differences from case to case.

A first difference hinges on whether or not the armed forces as such were directly responsible for most of the acts of repression. In those regimes which were scarcely militarized, such as Fascist Italy, Salazar's Portugal, or even Franco's Spain (where, despite its origins in a civil war and the prominent role this assigned to military officers, the government was progressively civilianized over the long period of the dictatorship), the most direct and "dirty" tasks were executed by a political police not formally subordinated to the military establishment. The latter may have "helped out" occasionally and looked on with sympathy, but its officers could claim not to have been directly implicated in such crimes. This facilitated their eventual acceptance of a democratic opening for two reasons: (1) they had less grounds for fearing revenge by civilian rulers, which would have affected their persons or their institutional integrity; (2) having intruded less into the administrative and functional apparatus of the state, they had a less traumatic adjustment to make in their individual careers or professional structures when ordered to return to their barracks.

In contrast, the cases of authoritarian rule in Latin America and Greece exhibit a more direct and unambiguous link between the armed forces and the commission of repressive acts. But here variations are also significant. Even where the separation between the political police and the military is, at best, unclear, there are cases—such as Brazil and Chile—where at least the dirtiest acts were committed (and in the latter case, are still being committed) by more or less specialized units within the armed forces. This prevents the military from merely feigning disgust and attributing to other agencies the "unfortunate" atrocities carried out, but it does exempt the bulk of military officers from charges of direct responsibility. The situation is worse in Argentina and Uruguay. There, repression reached levels equivalent to those of Chile, and much higher than those of Southern Europe (except those that followed the end of the civil war in Spain). Furthermore, such repression was the "institutional responsibility" of the armed forces—indeed, of many of its operative units. This makes it even more difficult for the bulk of the armed forces to disengage itself from the worst acts of the regime.

But we must take into account still other factors. One is the sheer magnitude and "quality" of physical repression—the degree to which particularly repulsive acts were committed, and the extent to which clearly innocent persons suffered. The more brutal, inhumane, and extensive were the repressive actions, the more their actual perpetrators—the institutions involved and those persons who collaborated in them or supported them—feel threatened and will tend to form a bloc opposing any transition. Where they cannot prevent the transition, they will strive to obtain iron-clad guarantees that under no circumstances will "the past be unearthed"; failing to obtain that, they will remain a serious threat to the nascent democracy.

This observation must be corrected by a more optimistic one, illustrated by the Spanish case. The passage of time attenuates the bitterest of memories, both of the regime's acts and of those of the opposition which "justified" the regime's atrocities. In such cases, those directly involved will have retired or been forgotten, and leaders of parties and groups representing those who suffered can invite all political actors "not to dig around in the past," as Santiago Carrillo, head of the Spanish Communist party, put it during a strategic moment in Spain's transition. This may calm the fears of those who might intervene to stop the transition, but in cases where the agents of repression are still very much alive and active, it will leave entrenched in important positions some of the most violent and dangerous protagonists of the outgoing regime—a point made forcefully in Alain Rouquié's chapter.

Thus, a policy of clemency would seem most viable and least dangerous for democratization where the repression was initially less brutal and extensive, or where it occurred a long time ago. Even so, the Spanish and Brazilian cases show the extreme sensitivity to this issue, and the ease with which it can threaten the transition or a recently consolidated democracy. Greece is another case in point. There, the authoritarian rulers committed a number of horrible crimes, but they were less repressive than the regimes of the Southern Cone of Latin America. Nevertheless, the succeeding civilian government had to rein in its stated intention to sanction all the military officers who had committed such acts, even where, as in contemporary Argentina, such a purpose was facilitated by the deep unpopularity of such officers following the army's military defeat in an external adventure. When the government of Karamanlis tried to condemn some important military figures, it limited itself to prosecuting a few—which led to accusations "from the other side" that it was perpetrating a "farce" that exculpated all the others. Nevertheless, this government found itself walking a tightrope over a series of attempted coups and assassinations. In other words, even a successor government as impeccably conservative and anti-Communist as that of Karamanlis had considerable difficulty in applying justice to what was almost a personal clique—embarrassingly defeated in war, moreover—of middle-level officers within the Greek armed forces.

Here we encounter yet another of the paradoxes that plague (and enervate) these transitions: where and when it is easier to bury the past, is where and when it is less important to do so. On the contrary, where these "past accounts" are of greater weight and more recent origin and involve a wider spectrum of persons, it is much more difficult and dangerous to attempt to collect them. Memories are more intense; victims (or their survivors) and victimizers are still present. Superficially this may seem to suggest that it is better (or at least more prudent) in such cases just to bury the past and to get on with the future. But this risks provoking justifiably indignant reactions, which may prove more difficult to cope with than the specter of a possible coup. We are here in a situation of most difficult ethical, as well as political, choice. Morality is not as fickle and silent as it was when Machiavelli wrote his expediential maxims of political prudence; transitional actors must satisfy not only vital interests but also vital ideals—standards of what is decent and just. Consensus among leaders about burying the past may prove ethically unacceptable to most of the population. All our cases demonstrate the immense difficulty of this dilemma;[16] none provides us with a satisfactory resolution of it.

But even under the worst of circumstances—heavy and recent occurrence, and heavy and widespread military complicity, as in contemporary Argentina—we believe that the worst of bad solutions would be to try to ignore the issue. Some horrors are too unspeakable and too fresh to permit actors to ignore them. Part of the cost of such a cover-up, as observed by Alain Rouquié in his chapter in Volume 3, would be to reinforce the sense of impunity and immunity of the armed forces, especially of the most sinister of its elements. A second cost is more diffuse but no less crucial. It is difficult to imagine how a society can return to some degree of functioning which would provide social and ideological support for political democracy without somehow coming to terms with the most painful elements of its own past. By refusing to confront and to purge itself of its worst fears and resentments, such a society would be burying not just its past but the very ethical values it needs to make its future livable. Thus, we would argue that, despite the enormous risks it poses, the "least worst" strategy in such extreme cases is to muster the political and personal courage to impose judgment upon those accused of gross violations of human rights under the previous regime. This requires due process of law fully guaranteeing the defendants' rights. No doubt, the first of such trials will be a traumatic experience,[17] but it is to be hoped that it can be made clear that judgments with respect to even widespread atrocities by military officers do not imply an attack on the armed forces as an institution.

What is even more fundamentally at stake in this issue is the change of the armed forces' messianic self-image as *the* institution ultimately interpreting and ensuring the highest interests of the nation—a conception, alas, even enshrined in the written constitutions of some countries. Such a conception, frequently linked to ideologies of "national security," implies that the armed forces should have an indisputable monopoly on determining what those interests are, and when and how they are being menaced. This, in turn, "commands" the military to intervene whenever it feels that some unacceptable ("subversive" or "antinational") party is about to come to power, that some intolerable degree of "disorder" or conflict has been reached, or that some vengeful force is about to act against the armed forces itself. The list of possible *casus belli* is long and varied—a tribute to the imagination, if nothing else, of the military and their civilian ideologues.

This reference to civilians reminds us of a crucial point: demilitarization is not a problem referring only to the military. The political tradition of the countries examined here has been plagued (and continues to be plagued) by civilian politicians who refuse to accept the uncertainties of the democratic process and recurrently appeal to the armed forces for "solutions," disguising their personal or group interests behind resounding invocations of the national interest; in no case has the military intervened without important and active civilian support.

How the messianic self-image of the armed forces' role and the manipulation of it by civilians can be transformed, is one of the key questions of the transition, and one which persists well into the phase of democratic consolidation. The answer depends not only upon whether and how certain actors are punished for their past transgressions, but also upon the lessons everyone draws from the authoritarian experience. We may be turning necessity into virtue, but it is important to note that many of the transitions examined here resulted from a traumatic and obvious failure of the preceding authoritarian regime. There is some reason to hope that in such cases quite a few actors will have been "vaccinated" against the temptation to pursue further authoritarian adventures, at least long enough (and here again, time and timing are crucial dimensions of our theme) for political democracy to emerge and take its first steps toward consolidation. Here we may have found—for a change—a fortunate paradox: the will to resist the temptation will be all the stronger the more resoundingly unsuccessful the previous authoritarian regime has been. Inversely, where the previous experience has been reasonably successful and, hence, where ensuing problems can be more credibly imputed to transitional or democratic rulers, the more likely it will be that actors will look back nostalgically (and selectively) to the "good old times" and be disposed to favor an authoritarian regression. This means, conversely, that a very negative evaluation of an obviously failed and highly repressive authoritarian experience, shared even by important segments of those who supported it, can be a subtle but important immunization against the risks and uncertainties that kind of transition is bound to face. Thus, if civilian politicians use courage and skill, it may not necessarily be suicidal for a nascent democracy to confront the most reprehensible facts of its recent past.[18]

Defusing (but Not Necessarily Disarming) the Military

We have suggested some necessary conditions for the armed forces to find and retain a "normal" institutional status within a functioning political democ-racy: they must somehow be induced to modify their messianic self-image; they must be given a creditable and honorable role in accomplishing (but not setting) national goals; and they must be made more impervious to the entice-ments of civilian politicians who turn to them when frustrated in the advance-ment of their interests by democratic means.

Only lengthy experience on the part of military officers presently on active duty and, especially, a concerted effort at educating future generations of recruits are likely to produce such a change in political behavior and expecta-tions. This cannot be called into existence just by some fortunate coalition of political forces or by some clever distribution of material payoffs. Rapid changes can be made in the juridico-formal definition of the military's role, such as redrafting constitutions and laws which assign it the role of sovereign adjudicator, or which link it to institutions other than those held by elector-ally accountable executives (e.g., commander-in-chief positions), but these are not likely to have much impact upon the deeply rooted self-images and attitudes of the officer corps.

There is also the issue of the armed forces' role in running state and para-state enterprises, a role that has been quite extensive in several of our cases (Brazil, Argentina, Peru, and Turkey). While this raises the prospect of milita-rization of the state and productive apparatuses, one could argue that such an engagement may be more positive than negative, especially where the armed forces play only a weakly credible role in the country's defense against exter-nal aggressors. Setting aside the question of whether, in a given society, offi-cers may be uniquely qualified for such managerial positions (a favorite theme of the North American literature on "the military in development" of the 1960s), one can observe rather cynically that such activities can be useful in occupying the time and interests of officers—active and retired—who might otherwise find little else to do. Moreover, this exposes those officers to a range of nonmilitary contacts wider than that provided by the unavoidable civilian "coup-inducers" discussed above. Even at the risk of increasing the danger—and cost—of corruption, such widening of civilian contacts may prove useful in diminishing the likelihood of a coup.

Again we find that we cannot advance further without drawing distinctions between the various situations represented by our cases. The form and pres-ence of the armed forces, as well as the nature of civil-military relations, differ considerably from country to country. At one extreme we find the most tradi-tional or "sultanistic" dictatorships, in which the armed forces are hardly more than the praetorian guard of the despot. Even if, as was the case in Nicaragua, they have modern arms, their professionalization is very low; as Max Weber pointed out, in these cases positions and lines of command depend on the whims of the *jefe máximo*, and the benefits of a military career come less in the form of salaries and institutionalized fringe benefits than in prebends allocated from above, or in payoffs extracted directly from the population. As the direct coercive agent of the despot, these military are difficult to distinguish from the ruling clique. They act more like armed bands than like armed forces. This makes it possible for revolutionary militias to mount a serious challenge to their monopoly of violence over a given territory. To this should be added that with the patrimonial, even "sultanistic," administration of the despot, and with the extractions of the military absorbing a large part of the country's economic activity, there tends to exist only a very weak native bourgeoisie. This pattern makes it most unlikely that a loyal opposition and a competitive political process will develop. In such cases, armed insurrection seems to be the only way for regime change and eventual democratization.

In the contemporary world, however, sultanistic dictatorships are exceptional cases. None are left in Southern Europe, and very few still exist in Latin America. Moreover, the interest of world powers in extending and stabilizing their "zones of influence" has raised the capacity of armed bands in these countries through military "assistance." They may still be far from professionalized armed forces, but they have made it more difficult for armed popular insurrections to succeed. Once the military has reached a minimal level of professionalization, only a severe rupture within it can open the way to a successful revolution. But even in such a case, the personalities and factions of the armed forces, allied with diverse parties and groups, are likely to become the principal protagonists (and antagonists) of the transition, as Portugal demonstrated in the aftermath of the 1974 "Revolution of the Carnations." But this happened under circumstances difficult to repeat elsewhere. First, as Kenneth Maxwell's chapter in Volume 1 makes clear, the Portuguese armed forces were in an unusual situation, due not only to their frustrated effort to defend the country's colonial empire, but also to their patterns of recruitment and promotion of officers. Second, even though the army's internal unity was broken by the putsch, there was no civilian insurrection in the metropole to challenge the armed forces' supremacy in the control of the means of violence.

In the other countries which concern us here, the armed forces are reasonably professionalized and have clear coercive supremacy within their territorial dominions. The regimes in which they find themselves (and which often they brought to power) are more formalized and depersonalized than patrimonial or sultanistic dictatorships. Moreover, there are local bourgeoisies with firm roots in the national productive structure. These features of the military and dominant classes make it highly improbable that the insurrectional route will be successful. In fact, attempts to impose a radical alternative by those means were crucial factors in the emergence of the authoritarian regimes whose eventual transition we are discussing (Argentina and Uruguay) or in the hardening of one already in place (Brazil). Our factual conclusion—stated above as a normative preference—is that for such countries the only route to political democracy is a pacific and negotiated one, based on initial liberalization and on the subsequent introduction of institutions of electoral competition, interest representation, and executive accountability—with the costs, trade-offs, and uncertainties such a course, as we shall see, entails.

Degree of Militarization of the Authoritarian Regime

The degree of military penetration of the polity and society varies across authoritarian regimes, as well as across the democratic ones that may follow them. The Franco regime may have been markedly military in its origins, but by the time of its transformation, the armed forces had become only one of several elements in what Juan Linz has called its "limited pluralism."[19] Portugal and Italy were even less military right from the start. At the other extreme, the Argentine regime of 1976 was governed institutionally by the armed forces, which designated the president, himself a high-ranking officer, who was in turn quite closely controlled by a military junta. Between these extremes, one can discern other combinations. For example, the authoritarian regime in Chile was originally headed by Pinochet as *primus inter pares* with fellow officers, but was gradually transformed into the personal dictatorship of Pinochet. Something similar occurred with Velasco Alvarado in Peru (1968–73) and Onganía in Argentina (1966–70). In the case of Brazil since 1964, the military have governed with a not insignificant civilian participation and without such a personalization of authority; moreover, high officers have rotated into upper executive office without incumbents always being able to control their succession. These differences have important consequences.

When the armed forces neither have nor feel a responsibility for the policies of the regime, it is easier for them to take a hands off attitude to the transition, by declaring themselves concerned only with protecting their own institutional values of stability and autonomy, as well as public order and national security. In such cases the armed forces can remain relatively indifferent to the emerging rules of the political game, the identity of partisan actors, and the content of policy demands. When the transition is initiated from regimes with extensive military participation, and especially where military officers remain as chief executives during the transition itself, the impact is more direct and immediate: the institutional interests of the military—not to mention the personal interests of the officers involved—cannot but be affected by emerging civilian authorities who may not be sympathetic to such considerations.

The situation is different when a *caudillo* has emerged from the pack to take personal command of the regime. Such individuals cannot imagine that the country could do without their services. In no case has a transition been initiated or guided by one of these *caudillos*. The only way out seems to depend either on the supreme leader's death (Franco and Salazar) or his overthrow (Onganía, Velasco Alvarado, Papadopoulos, and, perhaps soon, Pinochet). According to the latter scenario, the leader's colleagues arrive at the conclusion that his perpetuation in power poses a serious risk to them. Central to this calculation is the perception within the upper ranks of the armed forces that protracted exposure to the temptations and conflicts of government is causing an erosion of the military's professional integrity. Corruption is part of the problem, but the greatest concern centers on the politicization of the military establishment itself. Once a consensus forms within the armed forces that, in order for it to remain in power (i.e., to preserve its capacity to intervene in matters of importance to itself), it will have to get out of power (i.e., remove itself from direct responsibility for governing), the stage is set for a putsch aimed at transferring or surrendering political office to civilians. The more personalistic and concentrated power was in the authoritarian regime, the easier it will be for the putschists to make the ousted despot and his clique uniquely responsible for the failures and "excesses" of authoritarian rule, and the less they are likely to feel institutionally threatened by the subsequent transition.

Another factor encouraging a withdrawal from government concerns the agencies of repression. Whenever this "instrument" is used protractedly and indiscriminately, and whatever the initial formal engagement of the military, the units specifically responsible tend to develop an increasing autonomy and capacity to command resources. This exacerbates old rivalries between service branches and leads to skirmishes over jurisdictions and methods. Not only do the security agencies tend to prevail over more orthodox military units in such conflicts, but the very logic of their task leads them to apply their "skills" of surveillance, intimidation, interrogation, internment, and torture more widely, eventually to members of the regime itself (or to their friends and family members). The information they extract becomes an integral part of the regime's *arcanae imperii* and can be used to affect military promotions and lines of command. Faced with the growth of such a force in their midst, professionally minded officers may become willing to support a civilianization of authority which can deal effectively with such excesses. If such is the case, one imperative is that democratic civilians should accept (and encourage) in the armed forces the spirit of corporate professionalism that gave them the opening in the first place. This means following predictable and fair criteria with respect to promotions, while at the same time asserting the right of civilian authorities to control such appointments. Following such a policy is difficult since, on the one hand, the armed forces will be demanding decisional autonomy as a guarantee of their institutional interests and, on the other, some civilian political forces will be wishing to install individuals loyal to their aspirations in high military office, even if that means jumping ranks or appointing less professionally competent candidates.

The transitional regime and the eventual nascent democracy will also have to deal with the sensitive issue of military expenditures. During and immediately following the transition, there will be many competing claims for public funds and a generalized revulsion against materially rewarding the armed forces for what many are bound to feel is the mess they have made of civic life and, often, of the economy during the authoritarian period. It may even be tempting to disarm them or, at least, to scale down their salaries, perquisites, and equipment,[20] but this would conflict with the goal of encouraging professionalization—and it may trigger a violent reaction. We have not systematically inquired into the effects of a transition on military expenditures, but our impression from available evidence is that they tend to increase or, at least, not to decline. What seems crucial is not so much a crude buying off of the military as the devising of a shift in the strategic doctrines and operational capabilities of the armed forces which can provide them with a credible role in society—and that costs money.[21]

Our conclusion, then, is that there are conditional possibilities for coaxing the military out of power and inducing them to tolerate a transition toward democracy. The most difficult immediate problems are how to administer justice to those directly responsible for past acts of repression and how to assert some degree of civilian control over decisions about promotion and resource allocation within the armed forces. As we argued before, the longer-term issues—and hopes—involve a gradual change in the military's image of itself as ultimate guardian of the national interest and a shift from preoccupation with internal security to some more credible and orthodox role as defender of the country's (or the region's) external security.

While we are guardedly optimistic about the prospects for controlling the behavior of those within the armed forces who are antagonistic to democracy, the success of the transition may depend even more on whether some civilian, as well as military, leaders have the imagination, the courage, and the willingness to come to interim agreements on rules and mutual guarantees.

4 ·

Negotiating (and Renegotiating) Pacts

Pacts

The concept of "pact" emerged rather early in our discussions about possible transitions from authoritarian rule and was subsequently reiterated on many occasions. Only Terry Karl's chapter on Venezuela deals explicitly and thoroughly with such arrangements, but repeated pacts have also been an important feature of the Spanish transition. If Colombia had been included in our sample, we would have encountered more evidence for their crucial significance.[1] While we are not claiming that such arrangements are necessary features of a successful transition, we believe that they can play an important role in any regime change based on gradual installment rather than on a dramatic event.

A pact can be defined as an explicit, but not always publicly explicated or justified, agreement among a select set of actors which seeks to define (or, better, to redefine) rules governing the exercise of power on the basis of mutual guarantees for the "vital interests" of those entering into it. Such pacts may be of prescribed duration or merely contingent upon ongoing consent. In any case, they are often initially regarded as temporary solutions intended to avoid certain worrisome outcomes and, perhaps, to pave the way for more permanent arrangements for the resolution of conflicts. Some of the elements of those pacts may eventually become the law of the land, being incorporated into constitutions or statutes; others may be institutionalized as the standard operating procedures of state agencies, political parties, interest associations, and the like.

Otto Kirchheimer, who may have been the first to recognize the emerging importance of pacts in the contemporary world, pointed out that these compromises involve adjustments to standing contradictions between social content and political form.[2] Where the underlying distribution of de facto power in classes, groups, and institutions differs from the distribution of de jure authority, such arrangements permit a polity to change its institutional structure without violent confrontation and/or the predominance of one group over another. Moreover, he argued, the nature of these compromises was shifting away from the traditional liberal pact based on a strict delimitation of the spheres of civil society and the state, guaranteeing the individual right to dissent and the private privilege to own property, toward modern, "postliberal" pacts based on complex exchanges between public and private groups, mutually guaranteeing their collective right to participate in decision-making and their respective privilege to represent and secure vital interests.

Ironically, such modern pacts move the polity toward democracy by undemocratic means. They are typically negotiated among a small number of participants representing established (and often highly oligarchical) groups or institutions; they tend to reduce competitiveness as well as conflict; they seek to limit accountability to wider publics; they attempt to control the agenda of policy concerns; and they deliberately distort the principle of citizen equality. Nonetheless, they can alter power relations, set loose new political processes, and lead to different (if often unintended) outcomes.

At the core of a pact lies a negotiated compromise under which actors agree to forgo or underutilize their capacity to harm each other by extending guarantees not to threaten each others' corporate autonomies or vital interests. This typically involves clauses stipulating abstention from violence, a prohibition on appeals to outsiders (the military or the masses), and often a commitment to use pact-making again as the means for resolving future disputes. Certain national symbols and institutions (e.g., the flag, the anthem, holidays, uniforms, the monarchy, territorial integrity, international alliances, and federal structure) may also be protected against claims by "extremists." Pacts may also contain elaborate arrangements for regulating group competition (e.g., over members, voters, clients, and resources) and for distributing group benefits (e.g., positions of representation, cabinet offices, public jobs, career promotions, and budget shares).

Pacts exemplify a point made some time ago by Dankwart Rustow in a seminal article which has inspired much of our thinking on this point.[3] He argued that democratization advances "on the installment plan" as collective actors, each preferring a different mode of governance or a different configuration of institutions, enter into a series of more or less enduring compromises. No social or political group is sufficiently dominant to impose its "ideal project," and what typically emerges is a second-best solution which none of the actors wanted or identified with completely but which all of them can agree to and share in. Perhaps Adolphe Thiers—one of the founders of the French Third Republic, which came into existence by a single vote and lasted from 1875 to 1940—put it best when he said, "La République est le gouvernement qui nous divise le moins." A contemporary illustration of the ambiguity of such compromised beginnings of democratization is furnished by Spain, where the Right referred to the emerging regime as the result of a "reforma pactada," and the Left called it a "ruptura pactada," and both, so far, have learned to live with it.

The general scenario for negotiating a pact is fairly clear: it is a situation in which conflicting or competing groups are interdependent, in that they can neither do without each other nor unilaterally impose their preferred solution on each other if they are to satisfy their respective divergent interests. Subsequent changes in the relations between the actors and–especially in liberalized, partially democratized societies—the emergence of new actors who cannot be ignored and who desire to be "cut into" the game tend to change that scenario and impose the necessity of renegotiating, if not dissolving, existing pacts. We propose, therefore, to analyze this theme in terms of a series of temporary arrangements modifying rules of governance and mutual guarantees.

Let us first insist, however, that we do not regard pacts as a necessary element in all transitions from authoritarian rule—even in those which are gradual or continual. The outgoing rulers may be so discredited and in such disarray that it is not possible for them to negotiate with their successors. The authoritarian rulers may be compelled by pressure or anticipated reaction to abandon power without the exchange of mutual guarantees, the outcome being left open to the subsequent uncertainty of factional struggle or electoral competition. Conversely, the transition may be initiated from above by authoritarian incumbents with sufficient cohesion and resources to dictate the emerging rules of the game. Under these circumstances, their opponents must either acquiesce and compete under unilaterally determined conditions, or resist and risk being shut out of (or being victimized by) subsequent developments. Pacts are therefore not always likely or possible, but we are convinced that where they are a feature of the transition, they are desirable—that is, they enhance the probability that the process will lead to a viable political democracy.

It is tempting to conceptualize the transition as involving a sequence of "moments," to use Gramsci's expression: military, political, and economic. To each of these may correspond a different pact, or pacts, with a distinctive subset of actors negotiating about a distinctive cluster of rules.[4] The real world is hardly so accommodating, and actual transitions do not usually unfold through such incremental problem-solving; "moments" tend to overlap and confound each other. Nevertheless, while acknowledging that no empirical case exactly replicates our scheme, we will distinguish analytically between a series of possible *pactos*, each coming at a specific "moment" of the transition.

The Military Moment

The first moment focuses primarily on the military and involves the conditions under which they may tolerate some insignificant liberalization and begin to extricate themselves from direct responsibility for ruling. This sort of arrangement is irrelevant for those cases in which civilianization has already been accomplished under authoritarian auspices, for example, Spain and Mexico. Where the dictatorship is military and where the intent is to create some liberalized version of it (*dictablanda*), the crux of the problem seems to involve a prior concentration of executive power. Since the junta style of rule is the norm among contemporary bureaucratic-authoritarian regimes, some leader must emerge as capable of inspiring sufficient confidence among his followers to serve as guarantor for significant changes in power relations affecting military officialdom as a whole.

This *primus inter pares* ruler must then somehow find and empower valid interlocutors outside the regime itself, with whom to negotiate an extrication from government. It is difficult to predict who these are likely to be. Much will depend upon the effort previously expended to suppress parties, associations, and movements inherited from the preauthoritarian period, as well as the length of time which has elapsed before liberalization is attempted. Given the previous repression and disarticulation of intermediaries, "notables"—respected, prominent individuals who are seen as representative of propertied classes, elite institutions, and/or territorial constituencies and, hence, capable of influencing their subsequent collective behavior—seem to offer the best available interlocutors with whom to negotiate mutual guarantees. The basis of an extrication pact might well be the following: in exchange for restoring basic individual rights and tolerating some civic contestation over policy, the leader obtains an agreement from notables and/or moderate opponents that they will neither resort to disruption or violence, nor press too insistently or immediately their claim to govern, nor seek sanctions against military officers for "excesses" committed under the aegis of the authoritarian regime. Usually, the principal goals of such a liberalized dictatorship (dictablanca pactada) are to exert centralized state control over arbitrary and illegal acts of force by the armed forces, to prevent acts of vengeance against them, and to establish safe (if limited) channels for the articulation of interests and the discussion of policy alternatives. Such a compromise between military reassurance and political decompression involves a complex set of calculations. To be successful, the leader and his palace guard must retain the loyalty of the soft-liners, keep their former hard-line allies out of the main game,[5] locate and empower notables who can speak for and control their relevant constituencies, and inspire sufficient confidence among them to induce them to play the first rounds of the game according to the rules agreed upon.

If such a pact succeeds, liberalization and a not insignificant degree of civilianization may predictably ensue. But these developments are usually overtaken by the "resurrection of civil society," which we shall discuss below.

The Political Moment (or Moments)

The dynamics of the transition, plus the self-exhausting quality of an eventual pacto militar, imply that other actors and processes are likely to appear quite soon. This, in turn, suggests the possibility (but not the necessity) of a change in the nature of the compromises and in the identity of the actors entering into them, as new contradictions between social content and political form emerge. This time a pact would be based, not on a concentration of executive power and an arrangement of mutual guarantees with social and economic notables, but on a distribution of representative positions and on collaboration between political parties in policy-making. For reasons we will discuss below, the mobilization following initial liberalization is likely to bring political parties to the forefront of the transition and make the convocation of elections an increasingly attractive means for conflict resolution. At its core, such a pact involves a package deal among the leaders of a spectrum of electorally competitive parties to (1) limit the agenda of policy choice, (2) share proportionately in the distribution of benefits, and (3) restrict the participation of outsiders in decision-making. In exchange, they agree to forgo appeals to military intervention and efforts at mass mobilization. The capstone may be a "grand coalition" in which all the contracting parties simultaneously share in executive office, or a rotational scheme under which they (and no others) sequentially occupy it. But other, less rigid and visible, formats have also been imagined. Whatever the general format, the formation of such a "cartel of party elites" involves a certain amount of detailed, explicit—if often informal—institutional craftsmanship: an electoral law that discriminates against "unwelcome voters and/or unwilling parties"; a party finance arrangement that privileges contracting parties; a distribution of parliamentary districts and seats that protects the representation of minority members to the pact; a formula for apportioning public positions and budgets that ensures an "equitable" division of spoils; a restrictive policy agenda that guarantees the essential interests of supporters; a suprapartisan arrangement that deals with military affairs; and, finally, a commitment for some period to resolve conflicts arising from the operation of the pact by renegotiating its terms, not by resorting to the mobilization of outsiders or the elimination of insiders.

In the recent literature on democracy, this sort of pact is associated with "consociational" solutions to deep-seated ethnic, cultural, linguistic, or religious conflicts, and tends to be regarded as a stable, quasi-permanent form of democratic rule. Yet such arrangements might well be drafted to cover less communitarian cleavages, such as those of class, sector, region, institution, or even generation. As we shall see, it is not impossible that, via further pacts or ruptures, such formulas may last only for a while and then lead to a more egalitarian, individualistic, competitive, and broadly accountable democratic outcome.[6] However, our hypothesis is that pacts involving such coalescent and "cramped" behavior by dominant civilian party elites—pacts establishing limited democracy, or *democraduras*—will last longer than the military pacts which sponsor the transition to liberalized authoritarian regimes, or *dictablandas*. In the former case, the self-interest of participating party politicians and of established leaders of coopted subcommunities encourages the perpetuation of such cartels even after the initial conflicts and dangers which gave rise to such arrangements have diminished. *Self-perpetuating*

The succession problem which continues to plague even liberalized authoritarian regimes is resolved in democraduras by proportional adjustment, or by fixed rotation where there are presidencies. In any case, democraduras are protected from rapid swings in electoral popularity. In parliamentary regimes, subtle coalitional shifts may be sufficient. Regular elections and some opportunities for contesting policy may satisfy, at least for some time, minimal informational requirements for government responsiveness to meet changing demands and enough of the long-standing aspirations for citizen participation to ensure political peace. Therefore, unlike dictablandas, which are almost immediately transformed through the distinctively political process of liberalization, democraduras tend to be affected more by long-term changes in national socioeconomic structures and normative contexts, as well as by international political and ideological trends.

Subsequent socioeconomic changes may affect limited democracies in multiple ways. Growing individuation and secularization, coupled with increased social mobility and market vulnerability, undermine the capacity of contracting oligarchic leaders to control the behavior of their followers; voters will eventually become more free-floating in their preferences; association members will demand greater autonomy from partisan, ideological, religious, or cultural controls; new groups which cut across traditional cleavages will form; parties outside the pact may grow in strength and begin to play disruptive roles in parliament and cabinet formation. Under these circumstances, it will become increasingly difficult to hold the elite cartel together.

Limited democracies also have to cope with the fact that in contemporary times the normative standards of democratic theory and discourse do not correspond to the practices of such regimes. Citizen equality, majority rule, direct participation, parliamentary sovereignty, voluntary associability, accountable representation, unrestricted political choice, honest apportionment, public disclosure, *altérnance* between incumbents and challengers, and the like are not the usual practices of democraduras. The constitution and civil code may proclaim these rights, but their violation may be buried in administrative regulations, suffocated by informal norms, or masked by secret agreements. The transitional solution embodied by limited democracy, then, suffers a serious medium- and long-run legitimacy deficit when compared to regimes where citizens seem to be offered real opportunities to throw out incumbents and where leaders seem to be more truly accountable to mass publics.

As we have seen, one element motivating the search for an initial transitional pact is institutional decay within the military under the stresses (and personal opportunities) of direct responsibility for governing. In limited democracies it is the civilian apparatus of political parties, interest associations, and government agencies that is subject to decay. The guaranteed participation of these civilian elites in power and their stable share in the spoils of office, coupled with their protection from outside competition and from strict accountability to voters, members, or clients, are likely to produce complacency and corruption over time. These actors do not have to struggle continuously to stay in the game and to obtain significant rewards. Conformity to internal criteria of advancement within increasingly oligarchic institutions tends to become more important than responsiveness to demands from below or capacity to mobilize support. In short, the very success of such pacts can generate an organizational sclerosis that will deprive its contracting parties of their most crucial capacity—that of controlling the behavior of their followers.

When generalized disenchantment and institutional decay combine with policy disagreements within the elite cartel, some members of it may be tempted to ally with outsiders or to mobilize their followers to act in less conventional ways. Presuming that it proves impossible to renegotiate the relationship among the partners or to coopt opponents to join it, and providing none of the aggrieved parties resorts to (or succeeds in) bringing the military in on its side, movements toward a more thoroughgoing democratization of political life are likely to occur. The last restrictions on full political citizenship may then be removed.

The Wilson Center working group paid little attention to processes of consolidation and "advanced democratization" for the obvious reason that the cases and countries which preoccupied us were involved in the much more proximate and hazardous business of extricating themselves from various versions of authoritarian rule. But it seems relevant to sketch out how such a transformation might occur, if only because confidence that it can eventually occur may be a factor enhancing actor tolerance for more limited transitional forms. At other critical points of regime choice, we emphasized the role of possible pacts (if in some cases informal and even secret). They set the rules of the game, the continuing conditions, for political developments in the foreseeable future until, eventually, accumulated consequences make possible another change—an institutional breakthrough—in regime (or make change within the existing regime impossible).[7]

Movement toward more advanced forms of political democracy does not seem to require such explicit and multi-item renegotiations. Rather, it is more likely to occur through a sequence of piecemeal reforms, in response to a wide range of political pressures and policy calculations. Extensions of the franchise were perhaps the most visible and noisy of such modifications in the past, but by now that is almost an accomplished fact, even in most of the limited democracies. "Historic compromises," which bring long-excluded participants into partial governing responsibility, are another form of democratization for some polities. Elsewhere, the reforms are likely to be more discrete: changes in the electoral code and party finance statutes; more effective voter registration; more equal legislative apportionment; more transparent public information acts; greater administrative decentralization; lower barriers to party formation and parliamentary representation; dissolution of corporatist monopolies and obligatory associations; easing of citizenship requirements; and so forth. These are not dramatic changes in themselves, but their cumulative effect can be a substantial democratization of political life.

Some of these reforms may be associated with measures aimed at what we have called "social" and "economic" democracy: social security, state-provided health services, mandated sexual equality in employment, union recognition, worker representation in management, student participation in educational administration, children's rights, and so on. As Göran Therborn has pointed out, such "breakthroughs" in social and economic citizenship have often coincided with war or its aftermath.[8] In these cases, the advances in democratization did not involve a personal deal with a transitional leader or an institutional pact among political parties, but a diffuse agreement with the people compensating them for sacrifices demanded of them by the war effort.

Some American political scientists have argued that "critical elections" involving substantial realignments in the social bases of party support have provided an equivalent mechanism of democratic responsiveness in United States politics.[9] These seem rather modest accomplishments when compared with the accession to power of Social Democrats, Labourites, or Socialists in Western Europe, if only because it may take some time for actors to learn whether a lasting realignment has in fact occurred, and because the ensuing policy changes have been so limited. Roosevelt's New Deal should probably be considered the closest approximation to a turning point in democratization in the United States.

This scenario of democratization "on the installment plan," each stage laying down more inclusive and tolerant rules of competition and cooperation, is obviously a cautious, not to say outright conservative, transition path. Under such conditions, the Right is relatively strong and veto power remains largely and continuously in its hands. This has the advantage of tranquilizing the hard-liners of the nostalgic or reactionary Right and serves to differentiate them more clearly from the soft-liners, who progressively demonstrate their willingness to play politics according to procedural democratic rules; and it makes the spectrum of implicated actors wider than it would be if the transition were guided only by the authoritarian regime's "historic" opponents. This, in turn, lessens the fears of moderates that they will be overwhelmed by a triumphant, radical majority which will implement drastic changes in property rights, distribution of wealth, international alliances, military command structures, and so forth.

As already noted, the principal disadvantages of such sequential changes are twofold: one, they tend to make possible only marginal and gradual transformations in gross social and economic inequities (a point to which we shall return); and two, they foster disenchantment (desencanto was the expression we used in the working group for this phenomenon, having picked it up from the current Spanish political jargon) on the part of those who struggled for democracy in the expectation that it would bring them immediate benefits either in the form of control over the state apparatus or rapid, substantial improvements in the welfare of the actors and classes with whom they identify.

But the timing of the transition and the learning effects passed from one national experience to another may be changing the scenarios and accelerating the process to the point that, at least in contemporary Southern Europe, countries are moving toward full political democracy without pausing for "prudent" consociationalism or other such interim arrangements. Indeed, Spain, Portugal, and Greece have attained the hallmark of full political democracy in surprisingly short order. Parties previously excluded from power have won a subsequent electoral majority and been permitted to assume exclusive governing responsibility—something which has yet to happen at the national level in Italy, and which took several decades to accomplish in France. Undoubtedly, in these latter two cases, the presence of a large, well-established Communist party, which would have had to be included in the governing coalition, was a major factor in inhibiting such an alternation for a long time. Only once the Socialists became a demonstrably larger force than the Communists did this take place in France; Italy's party system has not yet met this crucial test.

The available experience from Latin America is ambiguous in this respect. Older transitions, such as those in Venezuela and Colombia, have been marked by a series of detailed and explicit pacts. As Terry Karl points out in her chapter in Volume 2, those arrangements have resulted in heavy social costs. But it should be noted that with the exception of Costa Rica (to which we shall return), all of the unpacted democracies existing at different times in other Latin American countries were destroyed by authoritarian reversals. It is worth noting, too, that the social costs of those democratic and authoritarian alternations have been as bad as or even worse than those of the pacted democracies of Venezuela and Colombia.[10] On the other hand, the transitions in the contemporary scene—those of Peru, Bolivia, Ecuador, the Dominican Republic, and Argentina—are characterized by the absence of political (and economic) pacts. The least that can be said about these cases is that the prospects of consolidation of their democratic regimes look less encouraging than those of Southern Europe. The present and future probable exception is Brazil, where what we term a "military pact" and a "political pact" were clearly, if not explicitly, made, and where an economic pact may still be likely. Aside from other characteristics already noted, what differentiates Brazil from the other Latin American cases is the relative success of its authoritarian regime and, hence, the firm and inordinately enduring control that its transitional governments have been able to keep on the process. On the other hand, the authoritarian regimes of Peru, Bolivia, Ecuador, the Dominican Republic, and Argentina (1972 and 1982) collapsed in total discredit with the armed forces profoundly demoralized and fractionalized. In contrast to Brazil, this meant that neither the transitional governments nor the armed forces could, as the Argentine generals said in 1972, "bring all parties to the table of negotiations." This does not preclude that, in an effort to salvage those shaky democracies, political and economic pacts may be attempted in the future—but this leads us away from the theme of democratic installation toward that of consolidation.

The Economic Moment

Getting the military back to their barracks and subject to civilian control and getting political parties to compete according to the rules of political democracy are sufficient achievements to ensure significant regime change. Increasingly, however, there is evidence that these accomplishments must be supplemented by another type of concertive effort: some sort of socioeconomic pact.

The reason for this is simply the increased role of the modern state apparatus, regardless of regime type, in economic and social affairs. To the extent that complex sets of collective actors have emerged to represent the class, sectoral, and professional cleavages intrinsic to capitalist social relations, it has become necessary to reach some agreement on how state agencies, business associations, trade unions, and professional organizations will behave during the transition and beyond it. Whether such a "social contract" can be agreed upon, and implemented, may have a major impact on the economy's performance at a time of considerable uncertainty over property rights, mobilized pressure for redistribution of benefits, and nervousness among external creditors, customers, and suppliers.

As the chapter by John Sheahan in Volume 3 points out, authoritarian regimes typically leave a difficult economic legacy. They often act as agents of transnationalization, opening the economy to foreign trade and investment, increasing its vulnerability to externally generated impacts, and heavily mortgaging future earnings to outside creditors. Those regimes may also have increased the scope of technocratic intervention, through government planning, monetary controls, and/or state ownership. Grandiose development projects, increased military spending, compressed wages, rigid adherence to fashionable economic doctrines and/or expensive foreign adventures are other facets of their legacy. Regardless of the magnitude of structural changes and the severity of the circumstances which characterize each transition, however, it is virtually inconceivable that the transitional incumbents will be able to postpone taking major social and economic decisions.

This is where the idea of a social and economic pact is particularly appealing. Yet, such a pact is probably more difficult to reach (and, above all, to make effective) than military or political pacts.[11] Trust and willingness to compromise may be less pronounced among class and sectoral actors than among politicians. The capacity of such negotiators to deliver the subsequent compliance of their members is problematic, if only because the outgoing regime may have systematically repressed unions and professional associations and sporadically manipulated organized expressions of business interests. It is problematic also because interest associations that emerge or are resuscitated in the aftermath of liberalization are likely to be highly politicized and fragmented along ideological and territorial lines. If there are any lessons to be gleaned from analogous efforts by consolidated political democracies at pursuing incomes and other "concerted" neocorporatist policies, it is that success depends on the presence of authoritative, monopolistic, and centralized class associations sharing a high degree of consensus about macroeconomic goals.[12] Neither condition is likely to obtain during contemporary transitions from authoritarian rule.

This is not to say that such efforts are doomed to fail entirely (as shown by the partial—and controversial—achievements of the Spanish Pacto de Moncloa and successor agreements), or that this kind of pact is essential for stabilizing a newly installed democracy. It seems crucial that, during the transition, a compromise among class interests somehow be forged to reassure the bourgeoisie that its property rights will not be jeopardized for the foreseeable future, and to satisfy workers and various salaried groups that their demands for compensation and social justice will eventually be met. Central to any such compromise is the institutionalization of representation rights and bargaining mechanisms to enhance the role of organized intermediaries. Employer associations and trade unions must recognize each other's rights to act autonomously in defense of their respective interests and to be present at multiple levels of consultation, from the shop floor to macroeconomic policymaking. These conflicting class agents must help each other to acquire a reciprocal capacity for governing the behavior of their respective members, or else the compromises they hammer out will be voided by the defections of opportunistic capitalists and intransigent workers.[13] Again, what is ultimately at stake in this form of implicit compromise and, eventually, formal pact is less the exchange of substantive concessions or the attainment of material goals, however much these may be in dispute, than the creation of mutually satisfactory procedural arrangements whereby sacrifices bargained away in the present have a reasonable probability of being compensated for in the future.[14]

Whether or not such undemocratic means of negotiating (and renegotiating) agreements will be compatible with a viable political democracy is not simply a function of whether the governments, political parties, and class associations can somehow reach and implement them. These efforts may be helped or nullified by the forces of civil society which tend to erupt in the aftermath of the initial steps toward liberalization. It is to this theme that we now turn.

5 ·

Resurrecting Civil Society (and Restructuring Public Space)

Triggering the Resurrection

The dynamics of the transition from authoritarian rule are not just a matter of elite dispositions, calculations, and pacts. If we have emphasized these aspects up to now it is because they largely determine whether or not an opening will occur at all and because they set important parameters on the extent of possible liberalization and eventual democratization. Once something has happened—once the soft-liners have prevailed over the hard-liners, begun to extend guarantees for individuals and some rights of contestation, and started to negotiate with selected regime opponents—a generalized mobilization is likely to occur, which we choose to describe as the "resurrection of civil society."

This revival has to be set against the background of the success of most authoritarian regimes in depoliticizing as well as atomizing their respective societies. By physical repression, ideological manipulation, and selective encouragement, they manage to orient most of their subjects toward the pursuit of exclusively private goals. Not infrequently, they are helped by the fact that their coming to power was preceded by periods of intense social conflict and political mobilization. Individuals may feel for a while relieved to be "free from politics" and satisfied in the pursuit of immediate, self-regarding goals. In effect, they tend to withdraw into private pursuits and set aside, prudently ignore, or even forget their public and political identities.[1] Citizenship becomes a matter of holding a passport, obeying national laws, cheering for the country's team, and, occasionally, voting in choreographed elections or plebiscites.

By trivializing citizenship and repressing political identities, authoritarian rule destroys self-organized and autonomously defined political spaces and substitutes for them a state-controlled public arena in which any discussion of issues must be made in codes and terms established by the rulers—give or take a few tolerated dissidents and some mavericks carefully ignored by the regime-controlled media. Only the most highly motivated individuals are prepared to accept the risks of acting outside this arena. Authoritarian rulers tend to interpret the ensuing lack of perceivable opposition as evidence of "social peace" among previously conflicting classes and of "tacit consensus" for their policies.

But once the government signals that it is lowering the costs for engaging in collective action and is permitting some contestation on issues previously declared off limits, these regimes quickly discover that the so-called peace and consensus were, at best, part of an imposed armistice. Former political identities reemerge and others appear *ex novo* to expand, beyond anyone's expectations, the public spaces the rulers decided to tolerate at the beginning of the transition.

Although we cannot provide hard data to prove it, our personal experience in having lived through several of these moments indicates that the catalyst in this transformation comes first from gestures by exemplary individuals, who begin testing the boundaries of behavior initially imposed by the incumbent regime. This leads to mutual discoveries of common ideals, which acquire enormous political significance just because they are articulated publicly after such a long period of prohibition, privation, and privatization. In the precarious public spaces of the first stages of the transition, these individual gestures are astonishingly successful in provoking or reviving collective identifications and actions; they, in turn, help forge broad identifications which embody the explosion of a highly repoliticized and angry society.

The Layers of an Explosive Society

No description of the forms that this explosion can take could expect to be exhaustive: it might involve the resurgence of previous political parties or the formation of new ones to press for more explicit democratization or even revolution; the sudden appearance of books and magazines on themes long suppressed by censorship; the conversion of older institutions, such as trade unions, professional associations, and universities, from agents of governmental control into instruments for the expression of interests, ideals, and rage against the regime; the emergence of grass-roots organizations articulating demands long repressed or ignored by authoritarian rule; the expression of ethical concerns by religious and spiritual groups previously noted for their prudent accommodation to the authorities; and so forth. But it may be useful to distinguish some dimensions or layers of this unexpected (and, in some cases, unprecedented) resurrection of civil society.

Usually, artists and intellectuals are the first to manifest public opposition to authoritarian rule, often before the transition has been launched. Their capacity to express themselves by oblique metaphors no doubt protects them, as does their membership in a de facto world system of cultural exchange. The talent and courage of poets, musicians, playwrights, novelists, and satirists poke holes in the regime's pretense of incarnating supreme "national values and virtues," often by subjecting this pretense to ridicule and humor. Certain artists—singers and actors especially—come to symbolize by their sheer presence resistance to the regime and the survival of alternative values. With the relaxation of censorship that accompanies the opening, these critiques become explicit and, with enthusiastic public acceptance, their articulation becomes immensely popular—and profitable, to the point that opposition to authoritarian rule can become a highly commercialized "growth industry" and therefore more difficult to suppress.

Those individual cultural and artistic expressions have close links with, and strong repercussions within, certain collectivities, such as universities, literary journals, scholarly reviews, professional associations, and research groups. Through these linkages previously forbidden themes are discussed in semipublic forums, and connections are made with analogous experiences elsewhere. Even such apparently trivial things as dress or gesture may become generalized acts of defiance. If these challenges fail to penetrate the levels where real power is exercised, they do succeed in corroding the normative and intellectual bases of the regime. The emperor begins to appear naked.

Other groups from a rather different segment of the population also take rapid advantage of liberalization. Those privileged sectors who were among the regime's earliest supporters and who, at least initially, were among its main beneficiaries may come to the conclusion that the authoritarian regime is dispensable.[2] They may feel that the regime has accomplished what it set out to achieve—that is, what *they* wished to do—and that by perpetuating itself longer than necessary, it is incurring the risk of social polarization and violent popular reaction. Where the regime has been a manifest failure, these actors simply feel that it is time to try something else. Some of the regime's policies may also be contrary to the ideals and interests of such privileged groups, whose feelings may range from moral revulsion at the corruption and widespread repression of the regime, to the materialistic calculation that policies "excessively" supporting international capital or state enterprises are closing off their economic opportunities. Once they begin to meet more freely and to share information without self-censorship or fear of denunciation, they may find unsuspected communalities of purpose and resentment. Hence, such relatively privileged groups begin to act like a de facto opposition. The sight of industrialists, merchants, bankers, and landowners complaining about government policy and even occasionally expressing a preference for "open elections" has the double effect of indicating that such dissent may be tolerated and that the regime does not enjoy the consensus it has claimed. Now the emperor is seen not only naked but also unaccompanied by his usual retinue.

This does not imply that privileged sectors are destined to be in the vanguard of the resurrection of society. Quite the contrary. They may have good reasons to fear that the transition will not stop at a point compatible with the contractual freedoms of the market or the cozy relationships they enjoy with the state apparatus. Nevertheless, their superior capacity for action, their lesser exposure to the risks of repression, and their sheer visibility assign them a crucial role in the earliest stages of the transition. These actors may even be deluded into believing they are leading a sort of liberal-bourgeois revolution.

But this illusion is quickly dispelled when other social sectors begin to react. First, the presumed leadership of privileged actors is usually challenged by another stratum which often also initially supported the regime—namely, independent and salaried professionals. For a variety of reasons, some of which are explored in Salvador Giner's chapter, the highly urbanized and bureaucratized societies of Southern Europe and Latin America have proportionately large middle sectors, with distinctive professional identities and norms. They are often organized in a variety of "orders," "colleges," and "institutes," some of them state sponsored. Usually, associations of lawyers, engineers, architects, physicians, psychologists, journalists, and social workers are politically quiescent and oriented around the defense of corporatist privileges. But with the opening, many of them turn to the articulation of broader issues, such as respect for the law or the sanctity of professional norms and welfare of clients, and begin to argue that satisfaction of those demands is contingent upon democratization of political life. Their discourses have the great ideological weight of being uttered by "those who know." Respectable authority is thus lent to the critiques of the authoritarian regime and to demands for democratization. Lawyers' associations criticizing the legality of authoritarian measures and demanding the rule of law, and groups of economists assessing the social and economic costs of regime policies—these are obvious cases in point. But even professions seemingly more removed from politics enter the emerging public arenas with powerful arguments. Thus, for example, psychologists try to assess the microconsequences of repression and censorship. Architects and urbanists turn their attention to the closing out or privatization of formerly public spaces, often carried out by regimes that fear the assembly of large numbers of persons. Data sources, book manuscripts, essays, and pieces of research which were prepared during the years of severe repression but which authors could not (or dared not) make public now emerge. These works supplement the statements of professional associations and political parties, some become best-sellers, and all inject new life into universities, bookstores, cafes, and other meeting places where critical discussion is now tolerated, de facto if not yet de jure. Thus, once the first steps toward liberalization are made and some dare to test their limits, the whole texture, density, and content of intellectually authoritative discourse changes, giving an enormous impulse to the demise of authoritarian rule.

But the middle sectors help the transition not only by means of associations bearing intellectual authority. There are other actors, also mostly of middle-sector origin, who lend to the transition the no lesser weight of moral authority. Human rights organizations, relatives of the victims of prison, torture, and murder, and often churches are the first to speak out against the more repulsive facets of the authoritarian regime. They do so in the midst of severe repression, when most other actors acquiesce to the regime or choose to ignore its atrocities. Human rights activists, a rather recent and more Latin American than Southern European phenomenon, take enormous personal risks and become outcasts in a society that is still largely disinclined—or too afraid—to listen to them. Private and public international support to those actors helps, because it raises the perceived costs of repressive action against them and makes them feel that they are not entirely isolated. In some cases, such as Brazil and Chile, important groups within the Catholic church rapidly and firmly committed themselves to those values. This was important, since it gave human rights activists some protection from the very institution that regimes professing to defend "Christian and Occidental" values had greatest difficulty in repressing. In other cases, such as Argentina, Bolivia, and Uruguay, the Catholic church (with few and noble exceptions) chose to ignore, when it did not attempt to justify, the atrocities of those regimes. This made even riskier and more remarkable the stand taken by lay human rights groups, by other churches, and even by isolated individuals, such as the now famous "Mothers of the Plaza de Mayo" in Argentina.

But irrespective of these differences, when the transition is launched, human rights organizations and activists emerge with enormous moral authority. This provides them with a large audience for their eloquent critique of the authoritarian regime, a critique that inevitably spills over to include political and social rights which only democracy can reliably guarantee.

The enormous impact and prestige suddenly enjoyed by human rights activists and organizations must also be understood in the context of another, subtle but crucial, phenomenon. This is what may be termed the recovery of personal dignity. After years of arbitrary rule, police brutality, and despotic treatment in so many social contexts—in other words, after years of deprivation of the basic attributes of citizenship—many demand and rejoice in liberalization. At such moments, helped by human rights activists, intellectuals, and artists, many discover that they, too, have been victims of the regime's repression. Thus, the rage of many who shortly before seemed to support the rulers' illusion of enjoying a "tacit consensus" becomes understandable. This condemnation of the regime is even more intense if, as is often the case, corruption has pervaded it and can now be publicly exposed. This converges with the discourses of professional associations and of human rights organizations to create a general climate of intense ethical rejection of the authoritarian regime.

But the greatest challenge to the transitional regime is likely to come from the new or revived identities and capacity for collective action of the working class and low-ranking, often unionized, employees. Not surprisingly, this is the area to which liberalization is extended most hesitantly and least irreversibly. Not only have the organizations of these actors been the focus of a great deal of "attention" by authoritarian rulers—either through outright repression or state corporatist manipulation—but the direct relations of these actors with their employers have been decisively affected by the regime's policies. Most of the authoritarian regimes in our sample of countries have deliberately favored bourgeois interests, especially those of its most oligopolistic and internationalized segments.[3] The net impact of such efforts on real wages and social benefits of workers varies from case to case. In most instances these declined from previous levels in absolute as well as relative terms, but in some cases this decline was "compensated" for by increases in paternalistic state benefits. In all cases, however, the discretionary power of management in production and distribution was drastically increased, and workers' preexisting rights to collective representation were curtailed or annulled.

It is therefore hardly surprising that an enormous backlog of anger and conflict accumulates during these authoritarian regimes and that, as soon as it becomes possible to do so, this results in an explosion of worker demands. Many such demands focus on matters of immediate satisfaction—higher wages, better working conditions, less arbitrary policies of hiring and firing—but others aim at creating (or re-creating) institutions for class representation: freedom of association, the right to strike, collective bargaining, representation at the shop-floor level, fair application of labor legislation, extension of unemployment and other welfare policies. No liberalization can avoid mobilization and conflict around these issues, to which we shall return in the next section.

Even this does not exhaust the layers of a reemergent society. Of particular importance in both Latin American and Southern European cases has been the literal explosion of grass-roots movements, most of which have been organized around narrowly circumscribed territorial domains (*barrios* or *parroquias*). The combination of the previous regime's policies of deliberate atomization, its destruction of networks of representation, and its emphasis on centralized and technocratic policy-making tends to create contexts especially propitious to such forms of popular associability once the aggrieved parties can dare to assemble, discuss common problems, and form more or less enduring organizations. Admittedly, they are often helped to do so by outsiders—priests and nuns, students, lawyers, social workers, party militants—and rarely do they form comprehensive networks. But what matters here is that they are numerous and that their internal processes are quite often highly participatory and egalitarian. This has important implications for the emergent political culture of the transition. There are suddenly a multitude of popular forums—however ephemeral some of them may prove to be—in which the exercise and learning of citizenship can flourish in deliberations about issues of everyday concern. The proliferation of such popular spaces forces policy-makers to pay attention to and expend resources on discrete and troublesome issues of urban life which the previous regime has either ignored or dealt with in an imperious and technocratic manner. Comprehensive social pacts or national-level policy reforms will not resolve such issues, and therefore, the emergent political process acquires elements of decentralization which may deepen its democratic roots.

All these changes—rapid, unexpected, and encompassing most of civil society—undermine the attempts by regime soft-liners to perpetuate themselves in government. Those changes also raise the perceived costs of the coup that, at those moments more than ever, the hard-liners would want to make.

The Popular Upsurge

In some cases and at particular moments of the transition, many of these diverse layers of society may come together to form what we choose to call the "popular upsurge." Trade unions, grass-roots movements, religious groups, intellectuals, artists, clergymen, defenders of human rights, and professional associations all support each other's efforts toward democratization and coalesce into a greater whole which identifies itself as "the people"—*o povo, el pueblo, il popolo, le peuple, ho laos.* This emerging front exerts strong pressures to expand the limits of mere liberalization and partial democratization. The fantastic convergence that this upsurge entails is frightening both to the regime soft-liners, who sponsored the transition expecting to control its consequences, and to many of their quasi allies, the moderate regime opponents, who expected to dominate, without such noisy interference, the ensuing competition for the highest positions of government.

But the popular upsurge during the transition is by no means a constant. Some countries seem to have largely missed that euphoric moment when a vast majority of the population feel bound together on equal terms, struggling for the common goal of creating not merely a new polity but a new social order. For example, we found relatively little evidence of its occurrence in Spain or Greece. Even in Brazil, where these phenomena have received much attention, they have been restricted to São Paulo and the Center-South— admittedly a major portion of the country, but even there they did not reach high levels and subsided quite rapidly. Portugal in the aftermath of the 1974 revolution represents the most extreme instance in our sample of such a spontaneous outpouring of egalitarian solidarity and enthusiasm. The diverse layers of an almost instantly activated and politicized civil society did interact, to support and stir each other to demand further extensions in what was called "o processo." Under this impulse, the transition was pushed far beyond liberalization, and at times, it even seemed to be moving beyond political democratization toward what we have called socialization. But by the fall of 1975, the popular upsurge had crested, and the transition had settled into a more predictable mold. In retrospect, its comparatively long persistence in the Portuguese transition seems to have been partially the product of successful choreography by the Armed Forces Movement (MFA). By the encouragement of urban demonstrations and the sponsorship of the "dynamization" program in the rural areas, these transitional rulers were able to take advantage of, and to prolong, what was initially a spontaneous, voluntary (and unexpected) mass response. Argentina has experienced two moments of popular upsurge and unity against authoritarian rule, one occurring before an announced transition (the Cordobazo and the ensuing events of 1969), and another—much milder, both in intensity and duration—after it had become clear that something was indeed bound to change (the period following the Malvinas/ Falklands fiasco). In Venezuela in 1958, the people rose in massive strikes which paralyzed the whole country and forced a surrender of power by Pérez Jiménez. Peru also saw a broad popular upsurge in the early 1970s, and this seems to be what is beginning to happen in present-day Chile.

Our cases suggest that the shorter and the more unexpected the transition from authoritarian rule, the greater the likelihood of popular upsurge and of its producing a lasting impact on the outcome of the transition. The element of surprise (and relief) that comes from signals that the incumbents are more vulnerable than they appeared to be, and the fact that choices about the emergent rules have to be made quickly, seems to contribute greatly to the spontaneity and generality of the upsurge. Given more time to think and act, various layers of society may discover serious divergences in their goals and in their preferred strategies of action. Their common identity as "the people" may, upon reflection or when faced with concrete policy choices, be fragmented by class, status, gender, religion, ethnicity, language, and generation, not to mention ideological belief and partisan allegiance. Hence, where the transition is controlled relatively firmly and protractedly by incumbents, the popular upsurge is less likely to occur, and where it does, it tends to be more confined in space and time. This, in turn, implies that in such cases the pressure for moving beyond liberalization is lower and that the form of democracy which may eventually be achieved will tend to contain more oligarchic elements, more "islands" of institutionalized inequality in participation and accountability, than is the case when regime incumbents are faced with a resurrected civil society coalesced into a highly mobilized *pueblo*. It also seems that the relative absence of this upsurge reduces the likelihood of a coup-induced regression, although where "power is with the people" and "the people are in the streets," the promoters of such coups are likely to hesitate before the prospect of provoking a civil war: witness in Portugal the half-heartedness of the Spínola coup of September 1974, and the confusion of the coup and countercoup in November of the following year.

The impact of the popular upsurge upon the transition is clearer than the conditions for its emergence. Where widespread and recurrent popular mobilizations have occurred in the past and have been suppressed by the advent of authoritarian rule, *and* where something like a subterranean network of preexisting associations, unions, movements, and parties persists behind the facade of "social peace," a strong popular upsurge is more likely to occur. Italy, Argentina, Chile, and perhaps Uruguay would therefore be more likely candidates for experiencing such a phenomenon during the transition.[4] Yet the cases of Portugal, Venezuela (in the 1950s), and Peru suggest a concurrent hypothesis: where popular mobilizations have not been a strong feature of the past *and* where the institutional structure of civil society has been weak (and kept deliberately so by protracted state corporatism and/or repression), a strong popular upsurge may also be facilitated. In such cases, the very absence of well-established political identities and the sheer novelty of the groups which emerge in response to liberalization may make it easier for individuals to identify as equals and for groups to temporarily avoid conflicts over which form of political organization is going to predominate.

In any case, regardless of its intensity and of the background from which it emerges, this popular upsurge is always ephemeral. Selective repression, manipulation, and cooptation by those still in control of the state apparatus, the fatigue induced by frequent demonstrations and "street theater," the internal conflicts that are bound to emerge over choices about procedures and substantive policies, a sense of ethical disillusionment with the "realistic" compromises imposed by pact-making and/or by the emergence of oligarchic leadership within its component groups are all factors leading toward the dissolution of the upsurge. The surge and decline of the "people" leaves many dashed hopes and frustrated actors. As we have already pointed out, many withdraw from intense activism and high idealism to the pursuit of private goals; some form "political ghettos" within which the ideals of more thoroughgoing social transformations are kept alive;[5] still others may go underground and resort to terrorist violence and even court the prospect of a return to repressive authoritarianism. Whatever the mix of responses, the popular upsurge performs the crucial role of pushing the transition further than it would otherwise have gone. But the disenchantment it leaves behind is a persistent problem for the ensuing consolidation of political democracy. In the process of structuring the options of the transitions and taming the popular sector, one event plays a more important and immediate role than all others: the convocation of elections.

6 ·

Convoking Elections
(and Provoking Parties)

Another Convergence

The announcement by those in transitional authority that they intend to convoke elections for representative positions of national significance has a profound effect. If their intentions are believed and if it becomes credible that voters will be reasonably free in their choice—that is, that existing and future parties will be free to compete by putting forth alternative candidates and that incumbents will *not* be free to count votes or eliminate candidacies as they see fit—then relations between contending factions and forces, inside and outside the regime, begin changing rapidly. This is because the prospect of elections brings parties to center stage in the political drama, a position of prominence that they are subsequently likely to occupy for some time. If there is ever a "heroic" moment for political parties, it comes in their activity leading up to, during, and immediately following the "founding election," when, for the first time after an authoritarian regime, elected positions of national significance are disputed under reasonably competitive conditions.

Prior to this, in the earlier stages of the transition, parties may have played little or no role. In the case of *démocratie octroyée*, where an occupation force sponsors the change from above, parties may not even exist, except in the minds of exiles or in the calculations of foreign powers. In the case of *démocratie à contrecoeur*, where the sponsors are the soft-liners of the authoritarian regime, their initial intentions are usually limited to some liberalization with elections scheduled for an undefined future and, then, for insignificant offices only—with or without officially sponsored parties. The resurrection of civil society, and in some cases, its coalescence into a broad popular upsurge, forces revisions in the originally envisaged timetable and scope of elections. This is even more the case when the transition itself has been practically imposed upon the regime by a strong, active opposition.

Political parties usually play a minor role in such mobilizations and pressures. As we saw, most of the effort is borne by unions, professional associations, social movements, human rights organizations, religious groups, intellectuals, and artists. Parties are frequently in too great a disarray, too divided, or too busy choosing their own leadership, to accomplish such a task. Indeed, one of the primary motives of transitional authorities in convoking elections for significant governmental positions may well be to get that multitude of disparate and remonstrative groups "off their back." In such cases, the authorities seem to hope that this will divert such activity into more orderly party channels, perhaps also calculating that by doing so they can divide and conquer their opponents. Moreover, they may hope that their magnanimous gesture will be so appreciated by the populace that their preferred party or candidate can win the ensuing contest.

In this last regard, the regime's expectations are frequently disappointed. Transitions are littered with examples of authoritarian soft-liners who overestimated their popular support: the Argentine military in 1973, the Brazilian generals in 1974, the Portuguese MFA in 1975, the Uruguayan junta in 1980, the Turkish military in 1983, even Indira Gandhi's failure to perpetuate emergency rule in India by electoral acclamation. However, expectations of channeling attention and activity away from the ebullience of civil society to the partisan structures of a more orderly political society have proven much more grounded.

Why this should be so is not difficult to understand. The electoral process has traditionally been organized along territorial lines. Indeed, this offers the only unambiguous criteria for delimiting constituencies in the contemporary world. No recent regime, no matter how corporatist its ideology, has managed to do away completely with territorial representation—if it tolerates organized representation at all—and party is *the* modern institution for structuring and aggregating individual preferences along those lines. The key to the party's efficacy in this regard lies in its capacity to generate symbols of partial political identity—around its name, platform, ideology, songs, logo, past and present leadership—which bring together voters and militants across many of the lines which otherwise divide them within society, whether class, status, family, gender, religion, ethnicity, language, or age. Moreover, since the number of elected positions is limited, the number of competing parties also tends to be limited. The sheer logic of putting together symbols capable of attracting sufficient votes and crossing the numerical threshold necessary for gaining representation ensures such a limitation—although the uncertainty intrinsic to founding elections encourages an initial proliferation of parties and candidacies, many of which subsequently disappear.

Once elections have been announced and seem likely to occur under reasonably fair rules, another peculiar convergence affects the transition. Regime opponents, provided they believe they have some chance of gaining representation, have strong incentives to cooperate with the regime's soft-liners, if only to guarantee that elections will be held. This frequently involves demobilizing radical or militant groups which may provide regime opponents with hard-core support, but whose actions—particularly those involving violence and "excessive" activism in the streets and work places—might discredit them in the eyes of more moderate potential supporters and/or jeopardize holding the elections at all. Thus, parties, whether revived or emergent (at least those who estimate having a good chance of obtaining representation), show themselves to be not only, or not so much, agents of mobilization as instruments of social and political control.

Moreover, the prospect of elections shifts attention to a new issue—namely, the definition of the rules under which the contest will take place. Usually, this is the first instance of the setting of more or less institutionalized parameters restricting the uncertainty of future outcomes.[1] Parties obviously have a strong interest in participating in the formulation of rules determining which groups are allowed into the contest, what boundaries constituencies will have, what criteria will be applied to determine winners, and so on.[2] For their chance to strike the best possible deal for themselves, given their calculations about the identity and location of their projected supporters, most parties are willing to pay a price. This price often involves entering into implicit compromises or explicit pacts with the transitional regime and with other parties and toning down their more militant supporters. This means that the basis of opposition tends to shift from expressions of principle to discussions of rules, and from demands for immediate benefits to pleas by political leaders to accept deferred gratifications.

compromise → traces of old regime

The Production of Contingent Consent

Where the rules are somehow successfully elaborated, they lay the basis for the "contingent consent" which underlies modern political democracy. Unlike classical democratic theory (which was based on the presumption of the ethical superiority of unanimity expressed by an assembled citizenry) or the theory of liberal democracy (which was based on the presumption that active citizens would elect and hold accountable individual representatives who would, in turn, produce substantively superior decisions through extensive public deliberation among themselves), contemporary theories of democracy place the burden of consent upon party elites and professional politicians (sporadically subject to electoral approval) who agree among themselves, not on ethical or substantive grounds, but on the procedural norm of contingency. These actors agree to compete in such a way that those who win greater electoral support will exercise their temporary political superiority in such a way as not to impede those who may win greater support in the future from taking office; and those who lose in the present agree to respect the contingent authority of the winners to make binding decisions, in exchange for being allowed to take office and make decisions in the future. In their turn, citizens will presumably accept a democracy based on such a competition, provided its outcome remains contingent upon their collective preferences as expressed through fair and regular elections of uncertain outcome.

The challenge in establishing such a political democracy is to find a set of rules which embody contingent consent. This "democratic bargain," to use Robert Dahl's expression,[3] varies from society to society depending on cleavage patterns and such subjective factors as the degree of mutual trust, the standards of fairness, and the willingness to compromise. Three dimensions, however, are likely to be crucial to all such efforts.

First, it is important to determine which parties will be permitted to play this game. During the transition, this poses the sensitive issue of how to treat parties which are avowedly "antidemocratic" or whose conception of democracy is not that of contingency. This issue also includes such seemingly technical matters as establishing thresholds for the representation of minor parties and/or for ensuring that certain social groups, especially minority ethnic or religious ones, should receive some guaranteed representation or protection.

The second dimension concerns the formula selected for the distribution of seats within constituencies, as well as the related one of the size and number of constituencies. Here the main choice is whether consent will be better produced by giving a "premium" to the party that receives the most votes, or by distributing the seats according to the proportionate vote totals obtained, or by a mixed formula that rewards majority parties in some constituencies while compensating minority ones in others (such as the complicated system adopted by the Federal Republic of Germany). The possible variants are, of course, quite numerous, especially when the possibility of a *double tour* is introduced. But in all cases, the underlying tension is between the desirability of creating "workable majorities" and that of producing "accurate representation." Other issues concern the drafting of rules concerning the size distribution of territorial constituencies and the intrinsic overrepresentation of agrarian interests in all spatially defined arrangements.

A third dimension in this nonexhaustive listing concerns the structure of offices for which national elections are held.[4] The two historical alternatives have long been parliamentarism, in which only representatives for subnational constituencies are voted upon (leaving aside the rare cases of countries organized into a single national constituency), and presidentialism, in which the office of highest executive power is filled by popular election (leaving aside the intricacies of electoral colleges in federalist systems). For a long time some countries (Finland, Ireland, and Iceland) have been practicing a mixed version of these formulae—semipresidentialism, as it is usually called—but only with the Gaullist constitution of the Fifth Republic in France has this possibility been seriously considered in new democracies.

Which combination of these choices will produce and subsequently reproduce contingent consent—a reasonable expectation on the part of winners and losers that they will be able to keep playing within the rules of democratic electoral competition? There can be no hard-and-fast answer to this question. Each national case has to experiment in order to find its own solution, and there is evidence from our cases that they are doing so. Giuseppe di Palma has argued that maximal inclusion of parties in the game, even of avowedly "extremist" parties, can overcome their resistance to democracy, and that extreme proportional representation and multiparty coalitional politics are preferable to efforts at creating a precocious majoritarianism or two-party rotation in power.[5] Juan Linz, in an unpublished essay, has made a convincing case that presidentialism jeopardizes democratic consolidation because it narrows available options, creates zero-sum situations, establishes single individuals in highly personalized and prominent office surrounded by excessive expectations, discourages the development of party organization and discipline, risks provoking a stalemate if parliament falls into the hands of an opposing party or parties, and reduces the flexibility of governments to respond to crises with shifts in personnel and policy.[6]

These seem valid arguments, and they all point in the direction of an Italian-style, ultraparliamentary solution. This would build in partisan diversity, decisional flexibility, sheer survivability, and eventually, political tolerance at the expense of protecting established socioeconomic interests, both by placing them out of reach of democratic accountability and by fragmenting representative institutions to the point that they are incapable of bringing sufficient state power to bear on crucial public issues. It is another matter whether those countries presently undergoing (or about to undergo) a transition from authoritarian rule, especially those in Latin America, with different political traditions, more pressing inequities, and less resilience in their civil societies, will find this a fair set of rules capable of generating contingent consent *and* attaining adequate performance. In any case, agreement on the rules alone is insufficient to ensure successful democratization. Much depends on the results which founding elections produce.

The Impact of Founding Elections

The results of democratic elections cannot be predicted from the rules under which they are conducted. If they could, they would not be democratic. In founding elections after a period of more or less protracted authoritarian rule, there are several reasons why this uncertainty of outcome is particularly high. For one thing, voters will have relatively little experience in choosing among candidates. Party identification will probably be weak and candidate images unclear, especially when the period of unrepresentative governance has been lengthy. Suspicion may make individuals wary of responding to pollsters. These factors may account for the unusually high percentage of "don't knows" and "undecideds" in all surveys taken before such elections. The ebullience of newly liberalized society is likely to produce big swings in enthusiasm and mood in the face of unprecedented and rapidly occurring events. One can therefore expect a good deal of "tactical voting." Some will wish to vote for candidates and parties that most decisively reject the previous regime, while others will prefer those which seem to offer the best bulwark against such a radical rejection. This jockeying around may be quite disconnected from longer-term class, sectoral, ethnic, and other interests. Add to this the probability of a tumultuous, if not chaotic, economic situation and one can imagine that not even the most skillful "psephologist" will be able to predict beforehand the distribution of electoral preferences. Those in power or close to it will make mistakes, usually by overestimating their support. Those outside it may well underestimate their capacity to draw votes from the population at large, and prefer to orient their efforts toward pleasing their militants and core clienteles.

Founding elections are therefore moments of great drama. Turnout is very high. Parties advocating cancellation, postponement, or abstention are swept aside by the civic enthusiasm that attends such moments. The results are scrutinized avidly and carefully. Moreover, founding elections seem to have a sort of freezing effect upon subsequent political developments. Where they are followed by successive iterations of the electoral process, few new parties get into the game, and many minor ones are likely to drop out. An examination of several founding elections in the past (France in 1848, Finland in 1907, Germany in 1919, Italy in 1948, and Japan in 1952) suggested that the distribution of voter preferences would tend to remain relatively constant for a while.[7] But the more recent cases of Portugal, Greece, and Spain have exploded that presumption. In these countries, the supposed freeze in partisan alignments quickly thawed, and there were remarkable vote shifts in subsequent elections. Unlike the earlier cases, where electorally induced alternations in government were slow to emerge (and have yet to happen in Italy and Japan), the contemporary Southern European cases show that rotation from "bourgeois" to Socialist party dominance (and vice versa in the case of Portugal) may come surprisingly quickly. Our impression is that this change is due largely to the fact that the modern state is much more closely coupled to the macroperformance of the country's capitalist economy than has been the case in the past. Voters are therefore more likely to punish incumbents, of the Left or the Right, for what they perceive as mismanagement of economic affairs. This produces a "pendular effect," rather different from the "critical elections" of the past, which sporadically and irreversibly shifted voter alignments.

Returning to the founding elections, we venture the following, rather paradoxical, and occasionally immoral observations about their outcome. For a transition to political democracy to be viable in the long run, founding elections must be freely conducted, honestly tabulated, and openly contested, yet their results cannot be too accurate or representative of the actual distribution of voter preferences. Put in a nutshell, parties of the Right-Center and Right must be "helped" to do well, and parties of the Left-Center and Left should not win by an overwhelming majority. This often happens either "artificially," by rigging the rules—for example, by overrepresenting rural districts or small, peripheral constituencies—or "naturally," by fragmenting the partisan choices of the Left (usually not a difficult task) and by consolidating those of the Center and Right (sometimes possible thanks to the incumbency resources of those in government).

The problem is especially acute for those partisan forces representing the interests of propertied classes, privileged professionals, and entrenched institutions, including the armed forces. We have argued that many of their vital interests are likely to be protected by the pacts which may accompany the transition, but, aside from the fact that such agreements are not always reached, this is unlikely to extract from those actors sufficient support for democracy. Unless their party or parties can muster enough votes to stay in the game, they are likely to desert the electoral process in favor of antidemocratic conspiracy and destabilization. Moreoever, where the Right collapses altogether and leaves the field virtually unimpeded to parties of the Left, the latter tend to fragment in short order, and their factions are likely to engage in efforts to outbid each other with more and more extreme promises to the electorate.

But in quite a few cases the electoral survival of the Right is an outcome by no means easy to ensure. These forces are themselves fragmented into hardliners nostalgic for a return to authoritarian rule and soft-liners often frightened by having been forced to convoke elections "prematurely." Moreover, the soft-liners, must bear the onus of their close association with the defunct regime,[8] and this makes it difficult for them to prove that they intend to remain faithful to political democracy. To do this, they may have to make concessions which negatively affect the interests of their supporters. On the other hand, if the rules are rigged too manifestly to favor the Right, the elections will be regarded as a farce and lose their "founding effect."

The dilemma for the parties of the Left is no less acute. In the nonrevolutionary transitions we are discussing, there is an asymmetry between the two camps. The Right must be prepared to sacrifice immediate material interests and be capable of overcoming its short-term symbolic disadvantage. The Left is called upon to underutilize its immediate symbolic advantage and to sacrifice, or at least to postpone for an undefined period, the goal of a radical, "advanced democratic" transformation. The Left too is likely to be divided into equivalents of soft-line and hard-line factions. The "maximalist" faction may be opposed to participating in elections per se, on the grounds that this will freeze existing political identities, divert energies to the terrain of procedural interaction and substantive compromise, and disillusion oppressed groups about the prospects for a radical breakthrough. On the other hand, "minimalists" of the Left and of the Center-Left face the risk that by not exploiting to the full their electoral advantage early in the transition, they may see that advantage evaporate in the future, as memories of heroic resistance to authoritarian rule fade and as other, better endowed, classes recuperate their organizational and symbolic supremacy. Minimalists may act "responsibly" at this stage, only to find that they have invested heavily in an electoral process which progressively marginalizes them.

Minimalists, if they are to avoid such outcomes, must make a substantial showing in the founding election. At least, they must be sufficiently indispensable in the subsequent deliberations over procedures and policies that their positions cannot be ignored, and they must be confident enough to withstand the criticisms of "treason" and "selling out to the system" that will be aimed at them by the maximalists. But if minimalists are too strong electorally, especially if they come to bear exclusive responsibility for governing, they are likely to have to cope, not so much with the immediate likelihood of a military coup, as with a major economic crisis. Capitalists, deprived of a reassuring presence in the electorate, wary of the efficacy of eventual pacts or constitutions guaranteeing their basic interests, and fearful that even centerist parties will have to escalate their substantive demands to cover their left flank, respond with the weapons they have closest at hand: disinvestment and capital flight.

One comforting element in this scenario for Center-Left and nonmaximalist leftist parties emerges where the Center-Right (or democratic Right, if it exists) wins the founding election and gains exclusive responsibility for the management of economic and social affairs. In such cases, the former can expect to reap the rewards of opposition in rather short order. Recent experience suggests that long-term dominance by conservative parties, Italian or Japanese style, is a thing of the past. The closer coupling of the economy and the state, the contagious effects of a more internationalized economy, and the higher level of external tolerance for democratic Socialist experiments suggest that alternation in government has become a more realistic likelihood. By playing according to the rules of contingent consent and initially accepting the role of strong but loyal opposition against Rightist governments doomed to suffer an erosion of support in the difficult aftermath of authoritarian rule, parties of the Center-Left and the Left may find—as the experience of Greece, Spain, and, in a rather more convoluted way, Portugal, suggests—that they have taken the best possible path to power, both in terms of optimizing their eventual electoral strength and minimizing the immediate risk that they would be impeded from taking office by violence.

7 ·

Concluding (but Not Capitulating) with a Metaphor

Transition in regime type implies movement from something toward something else. For the countries we have been concerned with, the initial something has been (or still is) authoritarian rule, although of differing social base, configuration, longevity, severity, intent, and success. The subsequent something else may be a political democracy, although present-day Turkey and the recent past of Bolivia, Argentina, and, in a different way, contemporary Nicaragua demonstrate that other outcomes are possible. In any case, the transition is over when "abnormality" is no longer the central feature of political life, that is, when actors have settled on and obey a set of more or less explicit rules defining the channels they may use to gain access to governing roles, the means they can legitimately employ in their conflicts with each other, the procedures they should apply in taking decisions, and the criteria they may use to exclude others from the game. Normality, in other words, becomes a major characteristic of political life when those active in politics come to expect each other to play according to the rules—and the ensemble of these rules is what we mean by a regime.

One major source of indeterminacy in the length and outcome of the transition lies in the fact that those factors which were necessary and sufficient for provoking the collapse or self-transformation of an authoritarian regime may be neither necessary nor sufficient to ensure the instauration of another regime—least of all, a political democracy.[1] These events and processes are, of course, interrelated and simultaneously present in any given historical process, but they must be analytically separated and evaluated. Factors that were of crucial importance in undermining a dictatorship, such as the conflict between hard-liners and soft-liners within the regime or the institutional decay of the military, become less relevant once new actors have been mobilized and the rules have begun to change. Inversely, aspirations and interests long thought to be eradicated or satisfied behind the previous regime's facade of "social peace" and "tacit consensus," for example, for local autonomy and class justice, may become major issues with which transitional authorities must contend. Some factors may change in sign, not just in significance. For example, an active, militant, and highly mobilized popular upsurge may be an efficacious instrument for bringing down a dictatorship but may make subsequent democratic consolidation difficult, and under some circumstances may provide an important motive for regression to an even more brutal form of authoritarian rule. On the other hand, conditions that are conducive in the short run to an orderly and continuous democratic transition, such as the drafting of interim pacts, may subsequently impede democratic consolidation if their restrictive rules and guarantees produce substantive disenchantment and procedural deadlock.

This is but another way of reiterating one of our opening observations: the high degree of uncertainty and indeterminacy which surrounds those who participate in a transition, both with respect to their short-term interactions and, even more so, with respect to the medium- and long-term consequences which ensue. It is not just that the actors are uncertain about the identity, resources, and intentions of those with whom they are playing the transitional game. They are also aware (or should be aware) that their momentary confrontations, expedient solutions, and contingent compromises are in effect defining rules which may have a lasting but largely unpredictable effect on how and by whom the "normal" political game will be played in the future.

To capture this situation, we propose the metaphor of a multilayered chess game. In such a game, to the already great complexity of normal chess are added the almost infinite combinations and permutations resulting from each player's ability on any move to shift from one level of the board to another. Anyone who has played such a game will have experienced the frustration of not knowing until near the end who is going to win, for what reasons, and with what piece. Victories and defeats frequently happen in ways unexpected by either player.

The analogy breaks down somewhat because transitional, multilayered, political chess is played by several, even by an unknown number of players, not just two. Moreover, the number of players is indeterminate rather than fixed at three. Nor are there necessarily such clear winners and losers, since in the transitional game players cannot only form alliances to protect each other's positions; they may also elaborate rules which have the effect of isolating certain parts of the board and of neutralizing the players' behavior with respect to these positions in such a way that their moves may have little or no effect upon the eventual outcome. In short, the risk of our exploiting the chess analogy is that the reader will imagine that we believe the transition process to be an orderly and cerebral game played by decorous and mild-mannered gentlemen. We ask the reader to conjure up a more tumultuous and impulsive version of the contest, with people challenging the rules on every move, pushing and shoving to get to the board, shouting out advice and threats from the sidelines, trying to cheat whenever they can—but, nevertheless, becoming progressively mesmerized by the drama they are participating in or watching, and gradually becoming committed to playing more decorously and loyally to the rules they themselves have elaborated.

To our knowledge, the game of multilayered chess has not been a commercial success. Nor would we expect our metaphorical one to endure. However indeterminate the initial moves of a regime transition may be and however uncertain the outcome may seem at the beginning, it is unrealistic to expect the game of politics to remain in such a state. In this sense the emphasis placed in Adam Przeworski's chapter in Volume 3 on uncertainty as *the* defining characteristic of democracy can be misleading. It is not the case, at least not in existing political democracies, that any player can get into the game, raise any issue he or she pleases, make any alliance he or she deems expedient, move to any level or into any area he or she feels concerned about, or take any of the opponent's pieces he or she can reach. The emerging practice of democracy institutionalizes "normal" uncertainty with respect to certain pieces and certain parts of the board, but in so doing it ensures "normal" certainty with respect to other pieces and parts of the board. Indeed, one could argue that democracy is a much better guarantor of some attributes—of rights to life, privacy, decency, movement, self-expression, "the pursuit of happiness," and private property—than are authoritarian regimes. The latter may lend some (often spurious) certainty to some aspects of the political game (e.g., who will occupy which executive positions and what policy decisions they will make), and they may have an awesome capacity to eliminate dissident players, but they do so at the expense of fostering considerable uncertainty outside a narrow political arena.

We have surmised that there are certain advantages if some authoritarian players, the soft-liners of the regime, believe that they are playing "white"[2]— that is, if they feel they are taking the initiative in most of the first moves during the transition. Furthermore, it is useful that players on the Right have at least the illusion that they have some significant control of the emerging game. No less useful seems to be the participation of all actors with significant pieces (i.e., political resources) in the game. Chaotic as it may seem to have several players attacking and retreating on various levels at once, it is better to have them in the game, and perhaps committed to its emergent rules, than outside it, threatening to kick over the board. In any case, as the game progresses (if it is allowed to progress), many of the frivolous, inexperienced, or overrated players will be eliminated or forced to align with others.

During the transition it is always possible for some contestants to kick over the board or, where authoritarian players still monopolize control over the pieces of organized violence, to remove their opponents by force. This, as we have seen, is a threat employed frequently in the opening rounds of the game but one which loses credibility the longer play continues and the more elaborate the rules become. Beyond a certain point, kicking or even pounding on the table may become counterproductive. It threatens one's allies almost as much as one's opponents, and the committed players may well join forces to eliminate the obstreporous one. What is more likely is that a number of initially enthusiastic players will withdraw from the game: the possibility of scoring a clear and quick win fades away; the benefits from playing along seem less and less worth the effort; the emergent rules prohibit certain moves and place out of bounds certain areas which were attractive earlier. The chess of democratic politics seems destined eventually to produce large numbers of kibitzers, cheering and mostly jeering the active players from the sidelines, but too discouraged by its complex rules or too alienated by its compromised payoffs to participate themselves.

The transition consists in inventing the rules for such a multilayered, tumultuous, and hurried game. Rules can be imposed unilaterally by a dominant actor and the other players may obey them out of fear or respect, or they can be elaborated multilaterally by implicit agreements or by explicit pacts. Rules may at some moment be packaged together into a single handbook—the constitution—but informal arrangements and norms of prudence are likely to supplement it (and occasionally to circumvent it). At a minimum those formal and/or informal rules cover the following points: what moves are permitted, what attributes authorize actors to be players, what assets entitle players to own which pieces, and what combinations of assets—what disposition of pieces—allow an actor or coalition of actors to control that central part of the board known as the government. If the game is reasonably democratic, the key attribute will be citizenship; the principal pieces will be relatively evenly distributed; the governing combination will be based on contingent consent among partisan leaders; and the substantive outcome of each round of plays— the policies of a government—will not be completely predetermined.

These procedural rules establish differing probabilities of winning and losing for specific players. Furthermore, at least in the transitional period, they are likely to be complemented by other rules which limit the game by placing certain parts of the board out-of-bounds, by prohibiting pieces of a certain color from entering the field of certain players, and by excluding certain moves without the agreement of all players. Pacts such as the one of Punto Fijo in Venezuela and those of La Moncloa in Spain are explicit examples of this sort of boundary maintenance between political and other social and economic institutions. But the same effect can be gained more implicitly by the establishment of neocorporatist systems of interest intermediation or consociational arrangements for respecting the autonomy of cultural-religious domains. The content and extent of efforts to remove substantive issues from the area of democratic uncertainty have been quite varied and will obviously differ according to the cleavage patterns of particular countries.

Nevertheless, once the transition has established the procedural rules of political democracy in the principal, overarching, and sovereign mechanisms of collective choice in a society, none of those restrictions is absolutely guaranteed to be respected in the future. Players, alone or in alliance, may subsequently move their pieces into initially restricted areas, by pushing liberalization into political democratization, and eventually by extending the latter into social, cultural, and economic institutions. The important difference is that such eventual extensions occur within the democratic norm of contingent consent, and not according to the authoritarian rules of personal whim or state security.

Irrespective of the idiosyncratic patterns and kaleidoscopic shifts within our sample, it is possible to offer a few generalizations to prospective players of our multilayered chess game. First, all previously known transitions to political democracy have observed one fundamental restriction: it is forbidden to take, or even to checkmate, the king of one of the players. In other words, during the transition, the property rights of the bourgeoisie are inviolable. This player may be forced to give up pawns and even be deprived of its rooks (e.g., the enlargement of the public sector, the expropriation of oligarchy-controlled land, and perhaps even the nationalization of banks), but its king cannot be placed in direct jeopardy. This is a fundamental restriction which leftist parties must accept if they expect to be allowed to play in the central parts of the board. Otherwise, they risk being eliminated, pushed to the margins, or reduced to the status of kibitzers. The second restriction is a corollary to the first, although it has its own autonomous basis: it is forbidden to take or even to circumscribe too closely the movements of the transitional regime's queen. In other words, to the extent that the armed forces serve as the prime protector of the rights and privileges covered by the first restriction, their institutional existence, assets, and hierarchy cannot be eliminated or even seriously threatened. If the armed forces are threatened, they may simply sweep their opponents off the board or kick it over and start playing solitaire. Beyond these two prohibitions, other agreements or impositions guiding specific transitions may guarantee the inviolability of other institutions (e.g., the civil service or churches), of other minorities (e.g., linguistic-ethnic subgroups or regional notables), and even of specific individuals (e.g., ex-presidents or ex-military commanders).[3]

During the transition there are likely to be actors who will refuse to play such a restricted game. They may refuse to forgo or postpone indefinitely their goals of abolishing the bourgeoisie and instituting socialism, or refuse to refrain from interfering with the military's command structure or with its role as guarantor of bourgeois property rights. If those actors are powerful enough to threaten the military's monopoly of organized violence, they run the risk of being forceably eliminated and/or of provoking a cancellation of the emergent game. Given the identity of players and the likely disposition of pieces on the board—the relations of force and influence—in the transitions that have concerned us here (with the exception of Nicaragua for the reasons already discussed), the only realistic alternative for the Left seems to be to accept the above restrictions and to hope that somehow in the future more attractive opportunities will open up.

One problem with transitions in countries where the bourgeoisie, and hence capitalism, is well implanted in societies of great inequality, and where the armed forces are strongly linked to such a skewed distribution, is that the game leaves few spaces and moves open for new players. The democratic forces, and not just those on the Left, may be allowed only a few weak and vulnerable pieces on the board. Much of their effort can be spent just moving around trying not to be taken. But here the phenomenon we described as the "resurrection of civil society" and, eventually, a strong popular upsurge are of crucial importance, since they may bring new, more varied, and impulsive players into the game, complicating the carefully laid opening gambits of regime incumbents. If the impulses from such processes do not lead to an authoritarian cancellation, then, even in societies as skewed as the ones referred to above, it becomes possible to open up additional spaces, so as to give some real interest and excitement to the game. This (partially) changed relation of forces, in turn, raises the possibility of more authentically democratic (implicit) agreements or (explicit) pacts, which reciprocally guarantee the assets of stronger and weaker players but do not entirely forestall moves toward alienating the more blatant or potentially more explosive social and economic inequities. In any case, however confused and multiple the number of initial players and their uncertain claques, the game will be consolidated in the hands of a smaller number of better organized actors with more reliable followers—essentially, recognized political parties and class associations. In such a case, it acquires more predictable rules and tends to concentrate on agreed-upon levels and areas of the board—those where the basic moves are electoral competition for filling specific positions and interest bargaining between organized class, sectoral, and professional groups for influencing public policy.

Political democracy, then, usually emerges from a nonlinear, highly uncertain, and imminently reversible process involving the cautious definition of certain spaces and moves on a multilayered board. Most moves aim at occupying the "center," where governmental institutions are located. Instead of using strategic positions in government as a basis for eliminating other players or for consolidating an impregnable redoubt, actors agree to occupy those spaces contingently and to share them with, or turn them over to, opposing players according to preestablished rules of competition.[4] This deprives players of many of their opportunities for maximizing interests and ideals, but does have the more prosaic virtue of "satisficing"—of obtaining some important satisfactions and avoiding the worst possible dissatisfactions. The configuration of that central space and the rules for occupying it differ from case to case, depending on the distribution of pieces at the start of the transition, the goals and assets of new entrants into the game, and the players' capacity to adjust their expectations and to reach compromises at critical junctures. Where political democracies are established gradually in societies with a dispersed and scarcely organized popular sector and weak political parties, the resulting space is usually highly restrictive and serves, at least temporarily, to ratify (if not to reify) prevailing social and economic inequalities. Where the popular sector emerges rapidly and as a relatively unified actor from liberalization or from the outright collapse of authoritarian rule, the issues and positions at stake tend to be more significant, including a more rapid transition to political democracy and even the possibility of movement toward socialization. If this is better from the point of view of our normative references, it has a negative side: such games run a greater risk of being cancelled during the transition, or even more so shortly after it, when their threatening potentialities become more apparent.[5] Such a cancellation can be done only by the player who, acting in defense of his own threatened pieces and/or of his bourgeois king, retains the ultimate capacity to kick over the board: the armed forces. But even in such high-risk cases, this is not an unavoidable outcome. If, as we have seen, the armed forces are in an advanced state of institutional decay and authoritarian incumbents are sharply divided into hard-line and soft-line factions, and if maximalists do not prevail in the opposition, there are opportunities for striking a "democratic bargain." Under such circumstances the bargain will tend to be more politically democratic and less obstructive of eventual future moves toward socialization than in cases where the popular upsurge has been weaker and the transitional regime has controlled most of the pieces and spaces on the board.

Nor is the game easy for opposition players. They are also likely to be fragmented into groups willing to accept different rules of competition and different institutional guarantees. Their most opportunistic elements will be willing to go along with whatever restricted space is offered them on the board. Their maximalist members may well seek to upset the whole board. Between these two is a vaguely delineated set of players. Let us call them "the democratic recalcitrants," who include the minimalists of the Left and Center-Left as well as other fringes of the Center committed to the instauration of political democracy. These actors will play only if the transitional incumbents are willing to negotiate with them a mutually satisfactory set of rules about moves, assets, and spaces. The main asset of recalcitrants is their joint commitment not to enter into a pact (*el pacto de no pactar*) too early and too easily with the regime incumbents, until restrictions they consider inherently antidemocratic have been lifted. Rather than attempting a specious democratization by violence, definitely withdrawing from the game, or passively accepting whatever terms the authoritarian rulers initially offer, recalcitrants seek to discredit those moves by incumbents in the eyes of national (and international) opinion. If this strategy is effective, and if the recalcitrants are believed to enjoy significant electoral support, the resulting elections will be predictably robbed of their "founding impact": this was true with the 1982 elections in El Salvador and with the various instances of Peronist abstention in Argentina. In such cases the transition will either have to start over or revert to an authoritarian mold. Therefore, democratic recalcitrants can affect the emerging rules, provided incumbents feel they must make concessions in order to gain credibility or electoral support. Another requisite is that recalcitrants must be able to control their own pieces. This may be an easier task for class-bound leftist parties than for populist ones with their loosely structured and heterogeneous clienteles. Where the latter emerge as dominant in the opposition, it may be quite uncertain whether, and to what extent, they will be willing and able to honor the rules and guarantees agreed upon with the incumbents. Thus, in spite of an ideological orientation which sounds more threatening than that of populist parties, the Right and Center may prefer to negotiate with class-bound parties of the Left.

Our analogy of the multilayered chess game entails two further implications. First, the players must be compelled by the circumstances of the transition to compete for spaces and pieces, rather than struggling for the elimination of opposing players; second, those players do not have to have attained a prior consensus on democratic values before muscling their way into the game. They can be made to respect the rules that emerge from the game itself. This is another way of saying that political democracy is produced by stalemate and dissensus rather than by prior unity and consensus. It emerges from the interdependence of conflictual interests and the diversity of discordant ideals, in a context which encourages strategic interaction among wary and weary actors. Transition toward democracy is by no means a linear or a rational process. There is simply too much uncertainty about capabilities and too much suspicion about intentions for that. Only once the transition has passed and citizens have learned to tolerate its contingent compromises can one expect political democracy to induce a more reliable awareness of convergent interests and to create a less suspicious attitude toward each other's purposes, ideas, and ideals.

Notes

Authors' Notes:

I want to express my gratitude for the support I received, first in the form of a fellowship from the John Simon Guggenheim Foundation and, thereafter, from the Ford Foundation. Without their help it would have been impossible to have found the time necessary to travel, to research, to write and at times to coordinate this project. I also thank Professor Candido Mendes and my colleagues at the Instituto Universitário de Pesquisas do Rio de Janeiro (IUPERJ) for providing the pleasant and stimulating milieu in which I did most of my work for this volume. At IUPERJ, Jorge Sapia helped me in my research. I wish also to thank the Helen Kellogg Institute of the University of Notre Dame for help and encouragement during the last stages of this project.

[G.O.]

I wish to thank the University of Chicago and, especially its Department of Political Science, not for any special material help they have given me in the project, but simply for being the sort of supportive and critical places they are. The hospitality of Guillermo O'Donnell and Cecilia Galli and the hard work of the staff of the Kellogg Institute of the University of Notre Dame—Julie Bixler, Rocio Gallegos, and Maria Walroth—were indispensable to the completion of this volume's final stages.

[P.C.S.]

Both of us wish to acknowledge the decisive role which the Latin American Program of the Woodrow Wilson Center for International Scholars and, most particularly, its founding secretary, Abraham Lowenthal, had in organizing and funding, as well as in helping us to conceive, the entire project. Our co-editor, Laurence Whitehead, helped us with his special insights and critical acumen, as well as with the coordination effort he accomplished during his stay as a Senior Fellow at the Wilson Center. Finally, the hospitality of the Center in providing this project, its authors, and its ideas with a receptive and creative "home" was due in no small measure to the support of its director, James Billington, and its co-director, Proser Gifford. It has been a long voyage across uncharted waters; we hope that all those who had a hand in the effort and those who read its product will agree that it was worth taking.

Chapter 2 Defining Some Concepts (and Exposing Some Assumptions)

1. This, in turn, obviously depends on how one defines "regime." By it, we mean the ensemble of patterns, explicit or not, that determines the forms and channels of access to principal governmental positions, the characteristics of the actors who are admitted and excluded from such access, and the resources or strategies that they can use to gain access. This necessarily involves institutionalization, i.e., to be relevant the patterns defining a given regime must be habitually known, practiced, and accepted, at least by those which these same patterns define as participants in the process. Where a regime effectively exists, real or potential dissidents are unlikely to threaten these patterns, owing to their weak organization, lack of information, manipulated depoliticization, or outright repression. For the purposes of summary comparison and generalization, these ensembles of patterns are given generic labels such as authoritarian and democratic, and occasionally broken down further into subtypes.

2. Our distinction between "liberalization" and "democratization" roughly parallels one drawn earlier by Robert Dahl between public "contestation" and "inclusion," although our emphasis on citizen equality and ruler accountability is somewhat different from Dahl's more passive notion of "inclusion." *Polyarchy: Participation and Opposition* (New Haven: Yale University Press, 1971). In chapter 3 of this book, Dahl explores the historical relationship between the two along lines rather similar to the ones developed herein.

3. Philippe C. Schmitter, "Speculations about the Prospective Demise of Authoritarian Regimes and Its Possible Consequences" (Working Paper no. 60, The Wilson Center, Washington, D.C., 1980).

4. Richard R. Fagen, "The Nicaraguan Revolution" (Working Paper no. 78, Latin American Program, The Wilson Center, Washington, D.C., 1981).

5. Dahl, *Polyarchy.*

Chapter 3 Opening (and Undermining) Authoritarian Regimes

1. The characterization of regime incumbents as "hard-line" and "soft-line"—as well as the similar distinctions we will later make between regime opponents—is a heuristic device designed to locate significant attributes of certain actors at different stages and conjunctures of the transition. These characteristics are not, therefore, permanent attributes of each actor, nor can they be assigned permanently to specific social groups or institutions; on the contrary, part of the plasticity and uncertainty of the transition consists in strategic changes within the ranks of both regime supporters and opponents. Nor are these attributes inherent psychological predispositions. Rather, they are meant to be inferred from the strategic behavior of specific actors as they confront the choices opened up by the transition.

2. For these themes and a more complete exploration of their interrelationships, see the chapter by Manuel Antonio Garretón in Volume 2.

3. This holds true even for the authoritarian regimes in our sample that were, by and large, more "successful," i.e., Spain and Brazil. In the former, extraordinary economic growth did not prevent the impending crisis of Franco's succession and the close relationship that this had with liberalization decisions. In Brazil, also in spite of extraordinary economic growth, factionalism within the armed forces, concerns of crucial military leaders about the expansion of the security apparatus, and protests from segments of the upper bourgeoisie at what they regarded as excessive expansion of the role of the state in the economy underlay the first liberalization decision. In line with our argument, it does not seem accidental that the Brazilian regime, one of the least crisis-ridden in our sample at the beginning of liberalization, has been the one that has maintained closer and more enduring control over the transition, although, as we shall see below, its relative initial stability is not the only reason for this.

4. For the initial formulation of the concept of "threat" as a crucial variable in the implantation of these regimes, and its reverberations over time, see Guillermo O'Donnell, "Reflections on the Patterns of Change in the Bureaucratic-Authoritarian State," *Latin American Research Review* 12, no. 1 (1978): 3–38.

5. The formula, however, has hardly been infallible, as is evidenced by the contemporary regimes in South Korea, the Philippines, and Indonesia.

6. The main source on this is Juan Linz and Alfred Stepan, *The Breakdown of Democratic Regimes* (Baltimore: Johns Hopkins University Press, 1978). For the Latin American context, the best source is David Collier, ed., *The New Authoritarianism in Latin America* (Princeton: Princeton University Press, 1979).

7. Linz and Stepan, *The Breakdown of Democratic Regimes.*

8. This expansion seems to us a crucial distillation of the differences we are sketching; contrast with the vivid portrayal by Juan Linz ("Crisis, Breakdown, and Reequili-

bration" in Linz and Stepan, *The Breakdown of Democratic Regimes*, pp. 3–124) of the "narrowing of the political arena" before the breakdown of democratic regimes.

9. A discussion of this case may be found in Guillermo O'Donnell, *El estado burocrático-autoritario: Argentina, 1966–1973* (Buenos Aires: Belgrano, 1982), forthcoming in English from the University of California Press. In his chapter in Volume 2, Marcelo Cavarozzi links that period with the more recent and much harsher authoritarian regime of Argentina from 1976 to 1983, as well as with a more global analysis of the past misfortunes of democracy in that country.

10. In the 1982 elections, the government party lost its majority in the Chamber of Deputies.

11. Albert Hirschman, *The Passions and the Interests: Political Arguments for Capitalism before Its Triumph* (Princeton: Princeton University Press, 1977).

12. Cf. Martin Needler, "Political Development and Military Intervention in Latin America," *American Political Science Review* 60, no. 3 (September 1966): 612–26.

13. Reference to Albert O. Hirschman, *Shifting Involvements: Private Interests and Public Action* (Princeton: Princeton University Press, 1982).

14. The original statement and a first exploration of these two "curves" is by Robert Dahl in *Polyarchy*.

15. Linz and Stepan, *The Breakdown of Democratic Regimes*.

16. Which may qualify it as one of the "insoluble problems" stressed by Juan Linz in "Crisis, Breakdown, and Reequilibration," pp. 50–55. The principal difference with the examples cited by Linz is that the one discussed here is a dilemma that simply cannot be avoided and one that the leaders must attempt to resolve.

17. Prudence suggests that those trials should be timed not to coincide with moments of electoral mobilization or mass protest, to avoid the appearance of "show trials" which would give an added motive for authoritarian regression.

18. For a more extensive treatment of how emerging democracies have coped with their dictatorial pasts, focusing on Germany, Japan, Austria, and Italy, see the essays in John H. Herz, ed., *From Dictatorship to Democracy* (Westport, Conn.: Greenwood, 1982).

19. See the classic paper by Juan Linz, "An Authoritarian Regime: Spain," in *Mass Politics*, ed. E. Allardt and I. Lithunen (New York: Free Press, 1970), pp. 251–83.

20. It may even be tempting to disband the armed forces altogether. Costa Rica accomplished this after the civilian uprising of 1948. The subsequent impact of this action upon democracy was positive, but it is doubtful, given today's international environment and the intervening development of military capabilities, that any contemporary transition could get away with such a bold step. The Bolivian experience following the revolution of 1952 was less fortunate in that, under the urgings of the United States, the armed forces were rapidly rebuilt, and it did not take long before they returned to recurrent coup-making.

21. De Gaulle's treatment of the French military after his turnaround on Algeria and the ensuing insurrection might be considered an object lesson in how to pacify and civilianize the armed forces, although we hope that none of the countries discussed here has the desire to acquire a *force de frappe*, its own capacity for nuclear deterrence. It is to be hoped that some less dangerous and expensive substitute can be found. For Portugal and Spain this has involved a greater and more integrated role within NATO; the Greek and Turkish military have been largely absorbed in their conflict over Cyprus and the Aegean.

Chapter 4 Negotiating (and Renegotiating) Pacts

1. The texts of these pacts—of Benidorm (1956), of the "Frente Civico" (1957), and of Sitges (1957)—are contained in Camilo Vázquez-Cobo Carrizosa, *El frente nacional*

(Cali:Carvajas, n.d.), and Jorge Cárdenas Garcia, *El frente nacional y los partidos políticos* (Tunja: Imprenta Departamental, 1958). For discussions of those pacts, see Alexander Wilde, *La quiebra de la democracia en Colombia* (Bogotá: Tercer Mundo, 1982), and Robert H. Dix, *Colombia: The Political Dimensions of Change* (New Haven: Yale University Press, 1967).

2. Otto Kirchheimer, "Changes in the Structure of Political Compromise," in *Politics, Law, and Some Exchanges: Selected Essays of Otto Kirchheimer*, ed. F. S. Burin and K. L. Shell (New York: Columbia University Press, 1969), pp. 131-59. We are grateful to Gianfranco Pasquino for having called our attention to the appositeness of Kirchheimer's work.

3. Dankwart Rustow, "Transitions to Democracy: Towards a Dynamic Model," *Comparative Politics* 2, no. 3 (April 1970): 337-63.

4. Rustow (ibid.) stresses the importance of a sequential logic in the establishment of political democracy, although his periodization and actors cover a longer time span than the one examined here.

5. Which may entail giving the hard-liners an unusual share of the substantive and symbolic rewards the regime can offer. The strategic problem is to keep them out of positions from which they could veto or reverse the intended process.

6. Indeed, in his recent summary of the consociational approach, Arend Lipjhart has extended it to cover countries which are not ethnically or culturally pluralistic (e.g., Colombia and Uruguay) and has admitted that, even where consociational regimes have been established for relatively protracted periods (e.g., the Netherlands and Austria), they may develop into other forms or types of democracy; see *Democracy in Plural Societies* (New Haven: Yale University Press, 1977).

7. Cf. Otto Kirchheimer, "Confining Conditions and Revolutionary Breakthroughs" in Burin and Shell, *Politics, Law, and Some Exchanges*, pp. 385-407.

8. Göran Therborn, "The Rule of Capital and the Rise of Democracy," *New Left Review* 103 (May-June 1977): 3-41.

9. The literature on "critical elections" is quite substantial, if largely confined to the United States. See V. O. Key, "A Theory of Critical Elections," *Journal of Politics* 17, no. 1 (1955): 3-18, for the initial idea. More recent treatments are Angus Campbell, "A Classification of Presidential Elections" in *Elections and the Political Order*, ed. A. Campbell et al. (New York: Wiley, 1960), pp. 63-77; Gerald Pomper, "Classification of Presidential Elections," *Journal of Politics* 29, no. 4 (1967): 535-66; and the principal historical study by Walter Dean Burnham, *Critical Elections and the Mainsprings of American Politics* (New York: Norton, 1970). For a more international discussion, see G. M. Chubb et al., *Partisan Realignment* (London: Sage, 1980), esp. pp. 19-47.

10. Costa Rica stands as the exception to this generalization, both in terms of stability of its regime and in terms of social equality (at least until the joint impacts of the international economic crisis and of the Central American wars provoked a serious economic crisis). This regime suggests that pacted democracies may not be the only safe path—although, as already noted, the Costa Rican governments have not been politically and economically saddled with a military establishment.

11. What is more, the socioeconomic pact may be bound together with the political pact, especially given the extensive attention that issues of economic management, worker rights, and social welfare have received in the drafting of modern constitutions, such as those of Italy, Portugal, and Spain.

12. For a recent and exhaustive treatment of the European experience with "social contracting" and its effects on incomes policies, fiscal compensation, indexation, price control, workers' participation in management, union bargaining, and more, see Robert J. Flanagan, David W. Soskice, and Lloyd Ulman, *Unionism, Economic Stabilization, and Incomes Policies* (Washington, D.C.: Brookings Institution, 1983).

13. On this point see Claus Offe and Helmut Wiesenthal, "Two Logics of Collective

Action: Theoretical Notes on Social Class and Organizational Form," *Political Power and Social Theory* 1 (1980): 67–115.

14. This theme is brilliantly discussed in Adam Przeworski "Rational Bases of Consent: Politics and Economics in a Hegemonic System," *Political Power and Social Theory* 1 (1980): 23–68, and Adam Przeworski and Michael Wallerstein, "The Structure of Class Conflict in Democratic Capitalist Societies," *American Political Science Review* 76, no. 76 (1982): 215–38.

Chapter 5 Resurrecting Civil Society (and Restructuring Public Space)

1. On this matter, see the discussion by Albert O. Hirschman in *Shifting Involvements: Private Interests and Public Action.*

2. This kind of movement from loyalty to the regime to "semi-opposition" or even outright opposition is categorized and described in the Spanish case by Juan Linz, "Oppositions to and under an Authoritarian Regime: The Case of Spain," in *Regimes and Oppositions*, ed. Robert Dahl (New Haven: Yale University Press, 1973), pp. 171–259.

3. During its first stage (approximately 1969–72) the Peruvian military regime was an interesting exception to this generalization. But it does not appear from Julio Cotler's chapter on Peru in Volume 2 that the efforts of military populists to change class relations from above were successful in relation to the working class.

4. The case of Italy was complicated by the protracted armed resistance to Fascism and German occupation that occurred after the 1943 downfall of Mussolini and surrender to the Allies. Perhaps this explains why in Italy, alone among the countries we are analyzing, the popular upsurge did not subside during the transition.

5. This has been the classic strategy of Communist parties when faced with electoral rules and popular preferences which assigned them to a minor electoral position. They typically respond by digging in at the local level in working-class neighborhoods and creating microcosms of a party-dominated social and cultural order.

Chapter 6 Convoking Elections (and Provoking Parties)

1. The granting of liberal rights to persons and groups usually precedes negotiations over the convocation of elections. This prior "concession" is, in most cases, unilaterally extended, since it involves no change in formal rules—most of what the authoritarian rulers have been doing is already against the constitution, the civil and criminal codes, etc.—but rather a promise to discontinue certain practices and to dismantle certain agencies. On these matters of rights, negotiation and formal compromise between political actors are rarely necessary.

2. This presumes that actors believe that rules elaborated for founding elections are likely to persist long enough to structure future contests. In countries where successive governments—not to mention regimes—have regularly changed the electoral legislation to suit their convenience, this may not be very credible. Argentina and Brazil, for example, have long histories of such manipulations.

3. Robert Dahl, *After the Revolution: Authority in a Good Society* (New Haven: Yale University Press, 1970).

4. For the sake of brevity we have chosen to ignore other types of rules, namely those concerning federalism, regional decentralization, or local autonomy. Obviously, the possibility of enjoying subnational office (and spoils) independently of whatever party controls national political institutions may be attractive in inducing losers to stay in the game, as well as in providing them with a better basis for eventually capturing national offices. In many countries the territorial distribution of authority has long been treated as a relative constant—to be inherited, in other words, by the transition. Contemporary

Spain demonstrates that this may not be the case, but decisions of this nature and magnitude are usually not dealt with at the same time as the initial electoral compromises.

5. We are indebted to the monograph by Giuseppe di Palma, "Party Government and Democratic Reproducibility: the Dilemma of New Democracies" (Working Paper no. 18, European University Institute, Florence, September 1982), for much of our sensitivity to this problem.

6. Juan Linz, "Stability and Regime Change" (Paper presented to the Committee on Political Sociology, IPSA-ISA, Werner-Reimers Stiftung, Bad Homburg, 18–22 May 1981).

7. This and the preceding generalizations are based on an unpublished essay by Philippe C. Schmitter, "Historical Bloc Formation and Regime Consolidation in Post-Authoritarian Portugal" (mimeo, University of Chicago, November 1978).

8. This is particularly true if authoritarian rule has ended—as happened in most of our cases—in resounding and widely acknowledged failure. As we observed above, the two reasonably successful authoritarian regimes, Spain and Brazil, managed to command respectable electoral support. Even in those cases the problem persists. This is shown by the recent overwhelming electoral victory of the PSOE in Spain, as well as by the enormous difficulties the PDS in Brazil faced, in spite of the government's manipulations of electoral and related laws, in order to retain its majority in Parliament and in the presidential electoral college.

Chapter 7 Concluding (but Not Capitulating) with a Metaphor

1. This should probably be called the "Stern Principle" in honor of Fritz Stern, who was the first, to our knowledge, to invoke it in its inverse sense, in differentiating between the fall of the Weimar Republic and the advent of National Socialism in Germany. Fritz Stern, "Introduction," *The Path to Dictatorship: 1918–1933* (New York: Anchor, 1966), p. xvii.

2. As expressed by Fernando H. Cardoso in our discussions.

3. Even though the outcomes of that "subgame" are, as Adam Przeworski argues, uncertain, the careful delimitation of that central space may well give the other restricted spaces—including the king of the game—what probably amounts to the maximum possible guarantee. In contrast, authoritarian regimes may enlarge the permissible spaces and moves in a more unpredictable, and hence less reassuring, way, even against those they claimed to be defending in the previous rounds of the authoritarian game.

4. As happened several times in Argentina and Bolivia, and—although under somewhat different circumstances—in Turkey.

5. See Rustow, "Transitions to Democracy."

Index

About the Authors

Guillermo O'Donnell is the Helen Kellogg Professor of Government and academic director of the Helen Kellogg Institute at the University of Notre Dame in South Bend, Indiana. His previous books include *Modernization and Bureaucratic-Authoritarianism: Studies in South American Politics.*

Philippe C. Schmitter is professor of political science at Stanford University. He is the author of *The Organization of Business Interests* (with Wolfgang Streek) and other books.

social
liberalism

economic
liberalism